A GUIDE TO WOMEN'S STUD IN THE OUTDOO

A Review of Literature and Research with Annotated Bibliography

Compiled and Edited by

NINA S. ROBERTS, M.A.

SIMON & SCHUSTER CUSTOM PUBLISHING

Cover Photo: Meryl Singer, a rock climber rappels down the sheer rock wall of the Hunchback arete high abov
the Santa Catalina Mountains, near Windy Point on Mt. Lemmon, which is just north of Tucson, Arizon.
Courtesy of AP/Wide World Photos.

Printed in the United States of America

10 9 8 7 6 5 4 3 2 1

ISBN 0-536-00782-9
BA 97549

 SIMON & SCHUSTER CUSTOM PUBLISHING
160 Gould Street/Needham Heights, MA 02194
Simon & Schuster Education Group

FOREWORD

Women have always been involved in the outdoors. This involvement has often been invisible, just like the research literature about girls and women in the outdoors. Nina Roberts provided an excellent service to individuals interested in the outdoors when she initially compiled an annotated bibliography about women's studies in the outdoors in 1991. Since that time, she updated this publication periodically and she now offers us the fifth edition of this resource. Nina asked me to write the foreword to this Guide to reflect on what this literature offers and to delineate the challenges in understanding the meanings of the outdoors for women and girls.

The adage, "you've come a long way," seems apropos when we examine the strides made by women (at least in Western countries) during the past thirty years. Yet, when we begin to examine what we know today about women and the outdoors that we didn't know 30 years ago, it becomes apparent that we still have a long way to go. This annotated bibliography includes almost 200 citations of literature and research studies published over the past twenty years. Yet, we know little for certain about girls and women in the outdoors. Many research gaps continue to exist.

I have written elsewhere about the evolutionary stages of research about women. These stages also apply to research on girls and women in the outdoors. In the first stage, we acknowledged the invisibility of information and knowledge about women in the outdoors that became apparent in the latter part of this century. This acknowledgment resulted in a second stage discussion of "women worthies" where scholars have attempted to identify women who contributed historically to the outdoor movement. In this second stage, we have seen literature about famous women's climbing teams and stories of women explorers. These stories have been important and significant, but they have not defined the relationship of women to the outdoors that most everyday women address. A third stage of the literature focuses on gender differences in the outdoors with the male model of outdoor experience generally compared to female ways of being.

Although these studies have made girls and women visible in the literature, they have not always helped understand the experience of women in new ways. The problem with this research is that the differences have become the conclusions rather the starting point for understanding the experiences of either males or females in the outdoors. A fourth stage of evolution in this field, concomitant with the gender differences stage, is research about the experiences of women. These studies are particularly useful in relation to understanding the value of women as leaders and of all female groups.

The newest emerging stage relates to an understanding of gender and diversity and how it effects women's and men's involvement and behavior in the outdoors, as well as elsewhere. Researchers are moving toward an understanding of gender and its meanings in the outdoors with some researchers beginning to acknowledge the great diversity that exists.

The literature in this bibliography represents two broad categories related to women's involvement in the outdoors: leadership and participation. Within both of these areas we see some studies, as well as essays and critiques, that address outcomes, constraints, and structures of involvement. This fifth edition of this Guide also reflects the growing number of individuals (both male and female) who are doing research about women. Many more researchers are needed. Although this volume includes only English language studies, the interest in women in the outdoors is growing worldwide. More opportunities for publishing research are needed for all kinds of outdoor studies.

You will find this collection of articles useful. We are learning about components of the outdoor experience for girls and women. For example, several studies have shown that all female groups in the outdoors are extremely valuable. What we don't know much about is how the dynamics of gender operate in any outdoor group. More research is needed. In addition, we need more theory based empirical studies. The outdoors can be a way that girls and women can resist traditional social roles, but it also can be a way that these roles are reproduced. Exploration of these topics requires more effort as we build a theoretical body of knowledge that will enable programmers to provide more inclusive programs for girls/boys and women/men, and enable researchers and educators to understand emerging perspectives about women's involvement in the outdoors.

KARLA A. HENDERSON, PH.D.
UNIVERSITY OF NORTH CAROLINA
CHAPEL HILL

SUMMER 1997

ACKNOWLEDGEMENTS

This project was conceived of and initially compiled during my summer 1991 internship with Woodswomen (Minneapolis), in conjunction with the graduate program at the University of Maryland, College Park. I appreciate responses to my phone calls and letters, and value the information received from several professionals around the nation; these contributions have helped build a strong foundation for this Bibliography. In particular, I'd like to thank Karla Henderson, Deb Bialeschki, Rita Yerkes, Susan Eckert, Deb Jordan, Mary Jo Kane, Wilma Miranda, Karen Warren, Betty van der Smissen and Martha Bell who represent a diversity of backgrounds and provided assistance integral to the completion and updating of this resource. Karla Henderson has been a pioneer in the field of women in recreation and has been instrumental in helping this project grow since the very beginning. Furthermore, I owe Karla a big thanks for her exceptional integrative review of this material. As a result, her essential contribution with regards to the Foreward of this '97 edition is greatly appreciated, and it provides all of us with a sense of where we are, and where we need to go.

Two other women deserve mention. Sherry Winn, graduate student at the University of North Carolina at Chapel Hill, assisted with additional data searches. I am grateful for her help in uncovering additional studies. Thanks to my mom (Colette) for sharing her artistic talent; cover design and sketches of women which follow are the result of her energy and support.

Special thanks to Denise Mitten, former Executive Director at Woodswomen, for helping to make this all possible. The continued support, encouragement and professional expertise from Denise is greatly appreciated. Also, her incredible insight helped constructively shape my thinking to assist with developing the introduction of this project. I sometimes feel that I can't thank her enough, not only for "coaching" me through the process of compiling this work, but especially for what I continue to learn from her. Thanks also to Denise, and Rita Yerkes, for their astute review of this work in preparation for publication. Sharon Heinlen, Executive Director of the Association for Experiential Education, also deserves a special thanks for her sharing her strength, and for constantly reminding me that this work is important.

* * * * * * * *

Final note: A portion of the proceeds for this bibliography are used to support the Women's Professional Group of the Association for Experiential Education. An investment in this guide, subsequently, has multiple benefits.

INTRODUCTION

Now in it's 5th edition, this resource guide is a compilation of research studies and papers about women in experiential education and recreation in the natural environment. The focus of this Guide is on adventure-based activities and physical recreation in the outdoors; therefore information regarding women in forestry, natural resources, and ecofeminism have not been included.

In 1991, during my graduate internship with Woodswomen, this Guide was merely an abstract thought while I was paddling a canoe in the Boundary Waters of Northern Minnesota. I envisioned how wonderful it would be to know about all the studies that have ever been done on women in the outdoors. The numerous "how-to" books, and stories about women's journeys, have paved the way and opened many windows. Yet, I soon realized that without a way to find the documented research, some of the doors were still closed.

Since the first edition was printed in 1991, this resource has been updated almost every year. During these last few years the amount of research being done on women's experiences in outdoor adventures and physical recreation has increased threefold, making subsequent editions of this publication more challenging. With the 5th edition, I have now begun to incorporate studies (written in the English language) which have been completed in other parts of the world. With the encouragement of Karla Henderson, my initial feeling that this task was overwhelming soon faded. There is a considerable overlap of scholarship and shared resources, and much to be learned and gained from reading the works of our sisters and brothers around the world. Karla taught me to believe it is important to begin including work from our international friends and colleagues. As a result, the newest goal for this annotated bibliography has been expanded to include a global perspective.

By updating this Guide, I continue to make a contribution to the growing discipline of women in the outdoors, as well as to the surge of studies on women and leisure as a whole. My hope is that this Guide of research studies will serve as more than an elaborate bibliography. The contents provide an overview of the diversity of experiences through which women in the outdoors mobilize themselves. This resource provides information about research which examines women as leaders and role models, topics of gender differences & traditional roles, feminist perspectives, experiential education and outdoor programming, wilderness challenges, group dynamics, individual differences, therapeutic adventures, and much more. This resource should also enlighten readers about the creatively varied programmatic approaches to the common goal of improving the social, economic and political status of women's participation in physical recreation and outdoor adventures. For individuals interested in conducting a research study of any extent, this Guide will serve as an invaluable tool. I want it also to provide a way for women (and men) to connect with others working on similar studies/programs, and serve as an invitation for increased networking among women from different ethnic and racial communities as well. The Author Index will be a catalyst in this process.

Historically, this Guide has included presentations from conferences and workshops. I have experienced increased difficulty in keeping up with the numerous topics being presented! Therefore, I've chosen to keep the few invited and refereed papers listed from previous editions in the bibliography section. This will provide you with a general sense of those subject areas which have been brought to a personal, interactive level within experiential education, outdoor recreation and related fields. However, this edition, and others in the future, will include work from presentations that have only been published in the respective conference proceedings. This will enable greater ease of access to the paper itself for anyone interested in obtaining a copy.

This fifth edition, with its chorus of voices reflecting the variety of topics flowing into women's outdoor experiences, represents an essential history as well as provides us with new directions for further change. Although this Guide is the most comprehensive resource of its kind available around the globe, it can be even more extensive through feedback from the vast community of individuals who work (or have an interest in) this subject. It is not exhaustive by any means. Because, for one, between the day I sent this Bibliography to the printer and the day it ended up in your hands another few projects will undoubtedly have sprung into existence. Secondly, as I begin to include work which is being done around the world, the databases grow larger and deeper. I intend, with your help, for this Guide to be as interactive and up-to-date as possible. For those of you who have conducted a study that is not included in this edition, fill out the brief questionnaire in the appendix and send it to me at the address indicated. Your study will be reviewed for consideration in the next edition. Those of you who know of other individuals that were not included, thanks for filling out the information sheet also in the back of this Guide. Send me the individuals' name and address, phone number, and or e-mail address — I will send them a questionnaire, or contact them by telephone or electronic mail.

Thanks to the women and men who devote their precious time, resources and scholarly talents in striving to improve the climate, acceptance and understanding of women in today's outdoor world and who, through this work, ensure that women and girls in generations to come will be welcomed into an environment (once dominated by men) that is far more equitable and appreciative of their talents and contributions. We have traveled a long way, yet our work is not over. More action is required, more empirical research is essential and, more female leaders and managers are needed. The authors and scholars represented in this Guide share a multicultural and diversified global vision of continued positive experiences for women in the outdoors.

NINA S. ROBERTS, M.A.
STUDENT CONSERVATION ASSOCIATION

AUTHOR INDEX

Listed below are the authors presented in this Guide. Most of these professionals have written and published numerous articles in a variety of areas. Included in the pages which follow are some of those with a specific focus on women in the outdoors. Many of these individuals have also been invited speakers nationwide as well as on an international level. A few of their invited and refereed papers are listed in the bibliography section under invited papers. If there are any authors included in this Bibliography who are not listed here, it is because no personal information was available at the time of this printing.

————————————————■•●●•■————————————————

Abromowitz, Jennifer: Author of Women Outdoors The Best 1900 Books, Programs, & Periodicals. Williamsburg, Massachusetts.

Appling, Leslie: Outdoor Instructor, National Outdoor Leadership School (NOLS).

Bean, Mary: Was pursuing a Master's degree at the University of Idaho in Wildland Recreation Management at the time her article was published. She is a certified scuba diving instructor.

Bell, Martha: Doctoral candidate, Department of Sociology, Massey University, Palmerston North New Zealand. Former Co-Chair AEE Women's Professional Group. Co-Founder Women Outdoors New Zealand / Aotearoa.

Bialeschki, M. Deborah: Associate Professor, Curriculum in Leisure Studies and Recreation Administration, University of North Carolina at Chapel Hill. She is Chair of the National Standards Board for the American Camping Association and of the World Leisure and Recreation Association Research Commission.

Blessing, Brenda Kay: Chairperson, Department of Health, Physical Education & Recreation at Missouri Western State College, St. Joseph, Missouri.

Burrus-Bammel, Lei Lane: Professor and Director, Service Learning Programs, West Virginia University, Morgantown, WV.

Chenery, Mary Faeth: Lecturer in the Department of Outdoor Education at LaTrobe University, Bendigo, Victoria, Australia. Former Professor in the Department of Leisure Studies at the University of Oregon, Eugene.

Cole, Ellen: Director, Master of Science in Counseling Psychology Program, Alaska Pacific University, Anchorage, Alaska. Former Dean in the Master of Arts Program at Prescott College in Arizona.

Drinkwater, Barbara: Chief of the department of ophthalmology of the U.S. Public Health Service Hospital and Clinical Associate Professor at the University of Washington Medical School in Seattle. Also an Associate Research Physiologist at the Institute of Environmental Stress.

Drogin, Ellen B.: Research Analyst for the Maryland-National Capital Park & Planning Commission. Also advises students in the Department of Recreation, University of Maryland at College Park.

Eckert, Susan: Founder and Director of Rainbow Adventures (Bozeman, MT), worldwide adventure travel vacations for women over 30.

Endres, Christine: Former Director of Camp Tapawingo for the Kickapoo Council of Girl Scouts, Inc. Relocated to upstate New York.

Estrellas, Anjanette: Adult Leadership Coordinator at the Institute for Intercultural Community Leadership at Santa Fe Community College. She is also a graduate advisor for the Master of Arts Program at Prescott College, AZ.

Freysinger, Valeria: Associate Professor, Department of Physical Education, Health, and Sport Studies, Miami University, Oxford, Ohio.

Griffin, Elizabeth: Assistant Professor of Recreation and Outdoor Education at Ithaca College in Ithaca, New York.

Groff, Diane: Doctoral candidate, University of Georgia. Former Assistant Director/Program Consultant at the Outdoor Institute in North Carolina; previous staff member at the Nantahala Outdoor Center in NC.

Hardin, Joy: Executive Director of Youth Educational Services (Y.E.S.), Humboldt State University, Arcata, California.

Henderson, Karla A.: Professor and Chair, Curriculum in Leisure Studies and Recreation Administration, University of North Carolina at Chapel Hill. A past-president of the Society of Park and Recreation Educators, the AAHPERD Research Consortium, and Academy of Leisure Sciences.

Holzwarth, Rachel: Founder and director of Alaska Women of the Wilderness Foundation. She is a shamanic healer, drummer, dancer and ritual artist.

Israel, Edie: Consultant in private practice in Boulder, Colorado and works for a Denver managed care company.

Johnston, Brenda J.: Research Assistant at the Institute for Outdoor Recreation and Tourism Studies. A division of the Forest Resources Department, Utah State University.

Jordan, Deb J: Associate Professor in the Leisure Services Division at the University of Northern Iowa at Cedar Falls, Iowa.

Kane, Mary Jo: Associate Professor and Director, Tucker Center for Research on Girls and Women and Sport. Distinguished Chair holder: Tucker Chair for Women in Exercise Science and Sport, College of Education and Human Development, University of Minnesota, Minneapolis, MN.

Kaufmann, Elizabeth: Former editor of Outside magazine. She covered the 1987 Snowbird Everest expedition for the Chicago Tribune.

Ketchin, Anne Forrest: Director, Environmental Studies Program at the Naropa Institute in Boulder, CO.

Kiewa, Jackie: Lecturer in Outdoor Education and Leisure Studies, Griffith University, Queensland, Australia. Her current research focuses on gender differences in the construction of identity (including values and attitudes) in climbing.

Koesler, Renà: Associate Professor in the Health, Physical Education, Recreation and Dance Department, Longwood College, Farmville, Virginia. A Wilderness Education Association (WEA) and National Outdoor Leadership School (NOLS) instructor. Past President of the Association of Outdoor Recreation and Education.

LaBastille, Anne: Wildlife Ecologist, Naturalist, and Author.

Lehmann, Katherine: Independent film producer and management consultant in Minneapolis, Minnesota. Her thesis pertaining to ethics and leadership was written during her graduate studies at the College of St. Catherine in St. Paul.

Lenskyj, Helen: Ontario Institute for Studies in Education.

Loeffler, T.A.: Assistant Professor, Memorial University of Newfoundland. Her doctoral dissertation, pertaining to career development in outdoor leadership, was completed during her graduate studies at the University of Minnesota.

Lynch, Pip: Lecturer, Department of Human and Leisure Sciences. Lincoln University, Canterbury, New Zealand.

McClintock, Mary: Freelance researcher/Better-Me-Than-You Research Services. Former Women Outdoors board member, and former Co-Chair of the Women in Experiential Education, a professional group of the Association for Experiential Education.

McCloy, Marjorie: Associate Editor, Women's Sports and Fitness magazine, Boulder, Colorado.

Mills, Judy: Lives in Montana Rockies, where she studies and writes about endangered species, exotic places, and adventurous women. Participated on an all-women trek through the Himalayas.

Miranda, Wilma: Associate Professor in the Department of Educational Leadership and Policy Studies at Northern Illinois University. Former co-chair for the Association for Experiential Education Women's Professional Group.

Mitten, Denise S.: Director of the Adventure Learning Center at Eagle Village in Hersey, Michigan. Former Executive Director of Woodswomen, Inc. in Minneapolis, Minnesota as well as a faculty member at Metropolitan State University in St. Paul.

Osius, Alison: Freelance writer and Senior Editor for *Climbing* magazine, Colorado. One of four women on the U.S. Climbing Team.

Paikoff, Roberta L.: Was pursuing a Master's degree at the Institute of Child Development, University of Minnesota at the time her article was published. Major research interests: adolescent development, self-concept, and women studies.

Pfirman, Elenore: Licensed Clinical Psychologist. Previous guide for Outward Bound and the Santa Fe Mountain Center.

Roberts, Nina S.: Assistant Director, Conservation Career Development Program of the Student Conservation Association. Chairperson of the Publications Advisory Committee for the Association for Experiential Education (AEE). AEE Board member.

Stripling, Sherry: Reporter/staff writer for The Seattle Times. Spent two months at the Everest base camp covering the 1988 Northwest American Everest Expedition.

Vesley, Carol: Department of Psychology, University of California at Santa Barbara.

Warren, Karen: Instructor in the Outdoors Program / Recreational Athletics at Hampshire College in Amherst, Massachusetts. Teaches graduate courses for Lesley College's National Audubon Expedition Institute.

Washington, Sharon J.: Project SPIRIT Director and Associate Professor, Department of Education, Springfield College. Former faculty in the School of Exercise, Leisure and Sport at Kent State University, Ohio. President of TapestryWorks (providing consultation on diversity, adventure education and organizational development).

Wesely, Jennifer K.: Her thesis pertaining to women, nature, and violence was completed during her graduate studies (M.S.) at Arizona State University in Tempe, AZ. Recipient of the Distinguished Achievement Award from ASU's Faculty Women's Association. Currently pursuing a doctoral degree in Justice Studies at ASU.

Yerkes, Rita: Dean and Professor, George Williams College, School of Physical Education and Recreation Administration at Aurora University, Aurora, Illinois. Co-founder of the Coalition for Education in the Outdoors, former Chair of the AEE Women's Professional Group, Past-president of the Association for Experiential Education.

A few men who have written about and studied women in the outdoors:

Birkett, Bill: Author; Award-winning photographer; International rock climber. His co-author, Bill Peascod, died of a climbing accident prior to publication of their book.

Bunnell, David E.: Institute of Environmental Stress, University of California at Santa Barbara.

Campbell, John B.: Department of Psychology, Frankin and Marshall College, Lancaster, PA

Ewert, Alan W.: Professor and Program Chair, Resource Recreation/Tourism at the University of Northern British Columbia. Former Branch Chief of the Recreation, Wilderness and Urban Forestry Research, USDA Forest Service.

Finkenberg, Mel E.: Professor and Chairperson of the Department of Kinesiology and Health Science at Stephen Austin State University in Texas.

Hessburg, John: Free-lance writer and staff writer for the Seattle Post-Intelligencer.

Hollenhorst, Steve: Assistant Professor of Wildlands Recreation at West Virginia University, Morgantown. His research and writing focus on social science aspects of natural resource management.

Kizer, Kenneth W.: Director of the California Department of Health Services and Assistant Clinical Professor of medicine at the University of California, Davis. He is a past president of the Wilderness Medical Society.

Knapp, Clifford: Professor of Outdoor Teacher Education at Northern Illinois University's Lorado Taft Field Campus in Oregon, Illinois.

Krakauer, Jon: Contributing editor to Outside magazine and author of a book on mountaineering.

Marsh, Herbert W.: Department of Educational Psychology, University of Sydney, Sydney, NSW 2006 Australia.

Schuett, Michael A.: Assistant Professor, Division of Recreational Administration, Department of Health, Physical Education, and Recreation, Southwest Texas State University, San Marcos, TX.

Stewart, William P.: Associate Professor, Leisure Studies Department at the University of Illinois (Champaign). Former Associate Professor at Texas A & M University.

BIBLIOGRAPHY

ABROMOWITZ, Jennifer

"Women athletes: A reference document for a course on the subject." (1977). Unpublished Senior Thesis. Hampshire College: Amherst, MA.

APPLING, Leslie

"Women and leadership." (September 1989). Proceedings of the NOLS Staff Conference, 9-12. Lander, WY: National Outdoor Leadership School.

BAKER-GRAHAM, Abigail

"Work with girls and young women at risk." (April 1994). Proceedings of a National One-Day Conference, *Adventure-Based Interventions* and a Study Weekend *Enabling Troubled Youth*. Ambleside, England, United Kingdom. (Available in ERIC Database, AN: ED378021).

BEAN, Mary

"Women in risk recreation." (Fall 1988.) *Women in Natural Resources,* 10(1), 26-28.

BELL, Martha

"Empowerment, competency and coercion: Experiences of pleasure and fear in a group of women outdoor instructors." (Fall 1996). In B. Baker (Ed.), *AEE Conference Proceedings*, (pp. 28-32). Spokane, WA: Association for Experiential Education 24th Annual International Conference.

"Feminists challenging assumptions about outdoor leadership." (1996). In K. Warren (Ed.), *Women's Voices in Experiential Education*, (pp. 141-156). Dubuque, IA: Kendall/Hunt.

"Feminism in the outdoors: Interviewing feminist women about their work." *Journal of COBWS Education*, 6(1), 22-29. (Canadian Outward Bound Wilderness School).

"Feminist outdoor leadership: Understandings of the complexities of feminist practice as women outdoor leaders." Master's Thesis (M.Ed.). Department of Adult Education, Ontario Institute for Studies in Education, (1993). University of Toronto, Canada.

BIALESCHKI, M. Deborah
Books

A leisure of one's own: A feminist perspective on women's leisure. (1989). State College, PA: Venture Publishing. See chapter 6, (pp. 108-110). (Co-authors: Shaw, S.M. and Freysinger, V.J., Senior author: Henderson, K.A.).

Publications

"Expanding outdoor opportunities for women." (August 1993). *Parks and Recreation*. (Co-author: Henderson, K.A.).

"We said `why not'? -- A historical perspective on women's outdoor pursuits." (1992). *Journal of Physical Education, Recreation, and Dance*, 63(2), 52-55.

"The feminist movement and women's participation in physical recreation." (1990). *Journal of Physical Education, Recreation, and Dance*, 60(1).

"Viva la diferencia!" (February 1987). *Camping Magazine*, 59(4), 20-22. (Co-author: Henderson, K.A.). Note: Abstract found under Henderson.

"Qualitative evaluation at a women's week experience." (Summer 1987). *Journal of Experiential Education*, 10(2). (Co-author: Henderson, K.A.). Note: Abstract found under Henderson.

"Outdoor experiential education (for women only)." (1986). In M. Gass & L. Buell (Eds.). *AEE Conference Proceedings*, (pp.35-41). Moodus, CT: Association of Experiential Education 14th Annual Conference. (Co-author: Henderson, K.A.). Note: Abstract found under Henderson.

Invited papers

"Negotiating constraints and women's involvement in physical recreation." Paper presented at the National Recreation and Park Association Congress (October 1995). San Antonio, TX (Co-presenters: Henderson, K.A.; Ainsworth, B.E. and Hardy, C.J.). Note: Abstract found under Henderson.

"Sports and outdoor recreation for women and girls: Issues and ideas." Paper presented at the National Recreation and Park Association Congress. (October 1994). Minneapolis, MN. (Panel presenters: Roberts, N.S., Mitten, D.M., Straw, S. & Thurber, K.).

"The invisible pioneers in leisure services: Women in the National Park Service." Paper presented to the American Alliance of Health, Physical Education, Recreation and Dance. (April 1991). San Francisco, CA.

"The meaning of physical recreation for women." Paper presented to the American Alliance of Health, Physical Education, Recreation and Dance. (April 1991). San Francisco, CA. (Co-presenter: Henderson, K.A.).

"Constraints on the physical recreation environment of women: An exploratory analysis." Paper presented to the Southeastern Women's Studies Association Conference. (April 1991). Charlotte, NC (Co-presenter: Henderson, K.A.)

"Women in leadership in the outdoors." Paper presented to the American Camping Association Conference. (February 1991). Detroit, MI.

"Outdoor experiential education (for women only)." Paper presented to the Association for Experiential Education. (September 1986). Moodus, CT. (Co-presenter: Henderson, K.A.). See publications.

"Experiential education from a female perspective." Paper presented to the American Alliance of Health, Physical Education, Recreation, and Dance. (April 1986). Cincinnati, OH (Co-presenter: Henderson, K.A.)

"Adult women and the camping experience." Paper presented to the American Camping Association Conference. (February 1986). Kansas City, MO (Co-presenter: Henderson).

"Women learning together in the outdoors." Paper presented to the National Women's Studies Association Conference. (June 1985). Seattle, WA. (Co-presenter: Henderson).

"Participant observation as a research technique for camping." Paper presented to the Research Section of the American Camping Association annual conference (March 1985). Atlanta, GA (Co-presenter: Henderson, K.A.).

BIRKETT, Bill
Women climbing: 200 years of achievement. (1989). London: A & C Black.

BLESSING, Brenda Kay
"Trait differences of women participants in selected levels of risk sports." Doctoral dissertation (Ph.D.). School of Health, Physical Education and Recreation. Ohio State University, OH. (1988). Dissertation Abstracts International, 49/04A. (University Microfilms Publication no. AAC8812229).

BUNNEL, David E.
"Caving practices, involvement in caving, and personality in NSS cavers: A survey study." (1985). *The NSS Bulletin; Journal of Cavers and Karst Studies*, 47(11), 51-57. (Co-author: Vesely, C.)

BURRUS-BAMMEL, Lei Lane
"Outdoor/environmental education   An overview for the wise use of leisure." (April 1990). *Journal of Physical Education, Recreation, and Dance,* see p. 52. (Co-author: Bammel, G.).

"Gender, sex roles and camping." (Fall 1983). *Women in Forestry,* 17-20.

CHENERY, Mary Faeth
"A magical place: YWCA Camp Westwind creates a mother-child camp." (February 1987). *Camping magazine, 23-26.*

CAMPBELL, John B.
"Sensation seeking among whitewater canoe and kayak paddlers." (1993). *Personality and Individual Differences,* 14(3), 489-491. (Co-authors: Tyrrell, D. and Zingaro, M.).

COLE, Ellen
Wilderness therapy for women: The power of adventure. (1994). New York, NY: Haworth Press. (Co-editors: Erdman, E. and Rothblum, E.D.).

DRINKWATER, Barbara
"Women on Annapurna." (1980). *The Physician and Sportsmedicine,* 8(3), 93-99. (Co-author: Piro Kramar).

DROGIN, Ellen B.
"The outdoor recreation experience: Factors affecting participation of African American women." (May 1993). *Journal of Experiential Education,* 16(1). (Co-author: Roberts, N.). Note: Abstract found under Roberts.

ECKERT, Susan
"Through the eyes of women in the wilderness." (1981). *The Creative Women,* 4(4), 4-7

ENDRES, Christine
"Women's outdoor equipment (or lack of it)." (Summer 1990). *Women Outdoors Magazine,* 10(4). (Article based on her Master's Thesis Research Project. Aurora University, Aurora, IL).

ESTRELLAS, Anjanette
"The eustress paradigm: A strategy for decreasing stress in wilderness adventure programming." (1996). In K. Warren (Ed.), *Women's Voices in Experiential Education,* pp. 32-44. Dubuque, IA: Kendall/Hunt.

"Understanding sexual trauma: A rationale and training manual for the experiential educator." Unpublished Master's Thesis (M.A.), Master of Arts Program, Prescott College, (1996). Prescott, AZ.

EWERT, Alan W.
"Group development through experiential education: Does it happen?" (1992). *Journal of Experiential Education,* 15(2), 56.

"Fear in outdoor education: The influence of gender and program." (January 1992). In K. Henderson (Ed.). *Research Symposium Proceedings*. Bradford Woods, IN: Coalition for Education in the Outdoors. (Co-author: Young, A.).

"Reduction of trait anxiety through participation in Outward Bound." (1988). *Leisure Sciences*, 10(2), 107-117.

"The identification and modification of situational fears associated with outdoor recreation." (1988). *Journal of Leisure Research*, 20(2), 106-117.

FIELDER, Erica
"Women and leadership." (March, April, May, 1979). *Women in the Wilderness Quarterly*.

FINKENBERG, Mel E.
"Participation in adventure-based activities and self-concepts of college men and women." (1994). *Perceptual and Motor Skills*, 78, 1119-1122.

FREYSINGER, Valeria J.
Books
A leisure of one's own: A feminist perspective on women's leisure. (1989). State College PA: Venture Publishing. See chapter 6, (p. 108-110). (Co-authors: Bialeschki, M.D., and Shaw, S.M, Senior author: Henderson, K.A.).

Publications
"A lifespan perspective on women and physical recreation." (January 1990). *Journal of Physical Education, Recreation, and Dance*, 48-51.

GOLDSTEIN, Judith E.
"Women striving: Pursuing the physical challenge." (January 1983). *Parks & Recreation*, 17(1), 71-81.

GRIFFIN, Elizabeth
"An interview with Dr. Anne LaBastille." (Spring 1982). *Outdoor Communicator*. The official journal of the New York State Outdoor Education Association, 12(5).

GROFF, Diane G.
"The effects of an outdoor adventure program on athletic team cohesion." (1989). Unpublished masters thesis (M.A.). Radford University: Radford, VA.

HARDIN, Joy
"Outdoor wilderness approaches to psychological education for women: A descriptive study." Doctoral dissertation. (Ed.D.). School of Education. University of Massachusetts: Amherst, MA. 1979. Dissertation Abstracts International, 40, 4466A. (University Microfilms No. 80-0934).

HENDERSON, Karla A.
Books
A leisure of one's own: A feminist perspective on women's leisure. (1989). State College, PA: Venture Publishing. See chapter 6, (p. 108-110). (Co-authors: Bialeschki, M.D., Shaw, S.M., & Freysinger, V.J.).

Publications
"Kind of in the middle: The gendered meanings of the outdoors for women students." (January 1996). In L. McAvoy, L.A. Stringer, M.D. Bialeschki, & A. Young (Eds.). *Coalition for Education in the Outdoors Third Research Symposium Proceedings* (pp. 94-106). Bradford Woods, IN. (Co-authors: Winn, S. and Roberts, N.).

"Expanding outdoor opportunities for women." (August 1993). *Parks and Recreation.* (Co-author: Bialeschki, M.D.). Note: Abstract found under Bialeschki.

"Breaking with tradition: Women and outdoor pursuits." (1992). (Editor/special issue). *Journal of Physical Education, Recreation, and Dance,* 63(2), 49-51.

"Women and physical recreation." (January 1990). *Journal of Physical Education, Health, Recreation, and Dance,* 61(1), 41-47. (Co-authors: Uhlir, G.A. and Greer, D.).

"Qualitative evaluation at a women's week experience." (1987). *Journal of Experiential Education,* 10(2). (Co-author: Bialeschki, M.D.).

"Viva la diferencia!" (February 1987). *Camping Magazine,* 59(4), 20-22. (Co-author: Bialeschki, M.D.)

"Outdoor experiential education (for women only)." (November 1986). In M. Gass & L. Buell (Eds.). *AEE Proceedings Journal.* (pp. 35-41). (Co-author: Bialeschki, M.D.). Moodus, CT: Association for Experiential Education 14th Annual International Conference.

Invited papers
"Negotiating constraints and women's involvement in physical recreation." Paper presented at the National Recreation and Park Association Congress (October 1995). San Antonio, TX (co-presenters: Bialeschki, M.D.; Ainsworth, B.E. and Hardy, C.J.).

"Constraints on the physical recreation of women: An exploratory analysis." Paper presented to the Southeastern Women's Studies Conference. (April 1991). Charlotte, NC. (Co-presenter: Bialeschki, M.D.).

"The meaning of physical recreation for women." Paper presented to the American Alliance of Health, Physical Education, Recreation, and Dance. (April 1991). San Francisco, CA (Co-presenter: Bialeschki, M. D.).

"Who were our mothers?: The invisible pioneers of the recreation movement." Paper presented to the NRPA Leisure Research Symposium. (October 1990). Phoenix, AZ. National Recreation & Park Association.

"Outdoor experiential education (for women only)." Paper presented to the Association for Experiential Education. (September 1986). Moodus, CT (Co-presenter: Bialeschki, M.D.). See publications.

"Experiential education from a female perspective." Paper presented to the American Alliance of Health, Physical Education, Recreation, and Dance. (April 1986). Cincinnati.

"Adult women and the camping experience." Paper presented at the American Camping Association Conference. (February 1986). Kansas City. (Co-presenter: Bialeschki, M.D.)

"Women in the outdoors." Paper presented to the National Women's Studies Conference. (June 1985). Seattle, WA. (Co-presenter: Bialeschki, M.D.)

"Participant observation as a research technique for camping." Paper presented to the Research Section of the American Camping Association annual conference. (March 1985). Atlanta, GA (Co-presenter: Bialeschki, M.D.).

HESSBURG, John
"Taking hold." (November 1985). *Pacific Northwest Magazine*. Special Issue: Women Who Climb - Their Search for Balance.

HOLLENHORST, Steve
Publications
"An examination of the characteristics, preferences, and attitudes of mountain bike users of the national forests: A preliminary analysis." (May 1993). Final Report prepared for the USDA Forest Service. Pacific Southwest Research Station, Riverside, CA (Co-authors: Schuett, M., Olson, D., Chavez, D.).

"Rockclimbers." (Fall 1988). *Women in Natural Resources,* 10(1), 15-17, 36.

Invited Papers
"Differentiating between early and late adopters in mountain biking." Paper presented at
the National Recreation and Park Association Congress LRS (October 1994), Minneapolis,
MN. (Co-presenters: Schuett, M., Olson, D. & Chavez, D.). Note: Abstract published in
the NRPA Leisure Research Symposium Book of Abstracts - found under Schuett.

HOLZWORTH, Rachel
"Outdoor programs for women: What they mean to women." (Winter 1992). *Women
Outdoors Magazine*, 13(1), 8-10.

HUMBERSTONE, Barbara
"Girls concepts of themselves and their experiences in outdoor education programmes."
(1991). *Journal of Adventure Education and Outdoor Leadership*, 8(3), 27-31. (Co-
author: Lynch, P.). Note: Abstract found under Lynch.

"Gender, change and adventure education." (1990). *Gender and Education*, 2(2), 199-215.

ISRAEL, Edie
"Treatment intervention with battered women." (Spring 1992). *NYSACD Journal*, 23-30.
(Note: Based on her dissertation, University of Northern Colorado, Greeley, 1989).

JAMES, Bill.
"Canoeing and gender issues." (August 1988). The Journal of Canadian Outward Bound
School, 4(1), 14-20.

JOHNSTON, Brenda J.
"Gender differences among intermountain West cavers, rock climbers, and hang gliders in
relation to psycho-social dimensions of constraint to participation." *Proceedings of the
seventh Canadian Congress on Leisure Research*, (pp. 213-216). (May 1993), Winnipeg,
Canada. (Co-author: Blahna, D.).

JORDAN, Deb
"Effective leadership for girls and women in outdoor recreation." (1992). *Journal of
Physical Education, Recreation, and Dance,* 63(2), 61-64.

"In the eye of the beholder: Perceptions of female and male outdoor leaders." (Sept. 1991).
Leisure Studies, 10(3), 235-245. (Note: This research was completed for her doctoral
study at Indiana University; abstract found under the reference for her dissertation).

"Snips and snails and puppy dog tails: The use of gender free language in experiential
education." (August 1990). *Journal of Experiential Education*, 13(2), 45-49.

"To dream the impossible dream: A leadership camp for young women in Iowa." (May
1988). *Camping Magazine,* 60(7).

"An examination of gender differences in perceptions of outdoor leaders by Colorado Outward Bound pre-registrants." Doctoral dissertation, (R.Ed). Department of Recreation, Indiana University, IN. (1988). Dissertation Abstracts International, 50/05B. (University Microfilms No. AAC8917750).

KANE Mary Jo
"Female involvement in physical recreation: Gender role as a constraint." (January 1990). *Journal of Physical Education, Health, Recreation and Dance, 52-56.*

KAUFMANN, Elizabeth
"Ascent of woman." (July/August 1991). *Women's Sports and Fitness*, 13(5).

KETCHIN, Anne
"Women out of bounds: An ethnography of outward bound as a symbolic experience." Doctoral dissertation. (Ph.D.). University of Colorado at Boulder. (1981). Dissertation Abstracts International, 42/08A, (University Microfilms No. AAC8200797).

KIEWA, Jackie
Publications
"The essential female adventurer." (1995). In C. Simpson & B. Gidlow (Eds.). *ANZALS Proceedings: Second conference - Leisure Connexions* (pp. 116-122). Canterbury, New Zealand: Australian and New Zealand Association for Leisure Studies.

"Body satisfaction and competence: Hand and glove?" (April 1996). *Social Alternatives*, 15(2), 7-10.

Invited Presentations
"Adventurous women: Motives, characteristics, constraints. A summary of research in progress at Griffith University." Paper presented at the National Outdoor Education Conference. (1995). Southport, Queensland, Australia. (Co-presenters: McIntyre, N. and Little, D.).

"Constraints and opportunities: Women's involvement in adventure recreation." Paper presented at the second ANZALS Conference, Lincoln University. (1995). Canterbury, New Zealand: Australian and New Zealand Association for Leisure Studies. (Co-presenter: McIntyre, N.).

KIZER, Kenneth W.
"Medical aspects of white-water kayaking." (July 1987). *The Physician and Sports Medicine*, 15(7), 128-132, 137.

KLARICH, Catherine.
"Gender differences in outdoor recreation participation in Whitman County." Master's Thesis, (M.S.). Department of Physical Education, Washington State University. (1995). University Microfiche No. GV181.3.K53.

KNAPP, Clifford E.
"Escaping the gender trap: The ultimate challenge for experiential educators." (Summer 1985). *Journal of Experiential Education,* 8(2), 16-19.

KOESLER, Rená
Publications
"Factors influencing leadership development in wilderness education." Doctoral dissertation, (Ph.D.). Michigan State University. (1994). Dissertation Abstracts International, 56/03A. (University Microfilms No. AA9524962).

Invited Papers
"Gender distinctions in leadership development." Paper presented at the Wilderness Education Association Conference. (March 1995). Fort Collins, CO.

"Leadership development for women in wilderness education." Fifth International Symposium on Society and Resource Management Conference. (June 1994). Fort Collins, CO: Colorado State University.

"Influences of leadership development among wilderness education participants." Paper presented at the Northeast Recreation Research Conference (April 1993). Saratoga Springs, NY.

"Opportunities and liabilities of female instructors." Panel presentation at the NOLS Fourth Annual Wilderness Education Conference. (September 1992). Sinks Canyon, WY. (Co-presenters: Byrd, C., VanBarselaar, L., Timmons, M., and Kearney, S.).

KRAKAUER, Jon
"High aspirations." (October 1990). *Women's Sports and Fitness,* 12(7), 32-36.

LABASTILLE, Anne
Women and wilderness. (1984). San Francisco, CA: Sierra Club Books.

LAINE, Kristen
"The Litmus Test: What works for women." (August 1987). *Climbing magazine,* 107-115

LEHMANN, Katherine
"Integrating ethics and leadership: A journey with Woodswomen." Unpublished master's thesis. The College of St. Catherine (1989). St. Paul, Minnesota.

"Connecting ethics and group leadership: A case study." (November 1991). *Journal of Experiential Education*, 14(3), 45-50.

LENSKYJ, Helen
Invited Paper
"Reflections on the female body, violation and empowerment in leisure studies research: The case of wilderness therapy." Keynote presentation at the Women and Leisure Conference (May 1995). Athens, GA: University of Georgia.

LOEFFLER, T.A
"Sexual harassment and experiential education programs: A closer look." (1996). In K. Warren (Ed.), *Women's Voices in Experiential Education* (pp. 213-225). Dubuque, IA: Kendall/Hunt.

"The current status of women's employment in outdoor leadership." (1996). In L. McAvoy (Ed.), Coalition for Education in the Outdoors, *Third Biennial Research Symposium Proceedings*, 107-115.

"Factors influencing women's outdoor leadership career development." (1995). *Melpomene Journal*, 14(3), 15-21.

"Women's career development in outdoor leadership." (1995). *AEE Conference Proceedings* (pp. 156-161). Lake Geneva, WI: Association of Experiential Education 23rd Annual International Conference.

"Factors which influence women's career development in outdoor leadership." Doctoral dissertation, (Ph.D.). Department of Recreation, Park and Leisure Studies. The University of Minnesota (1995). Minneapolis, MN. Dissertation Abstracts International, Microfilm No. 9541337.

"Leading the way: Rockclimbing instruction for women." Master's thesis, (M.S.). Experiential Education Department. Mankato State University (1991). Mankato, MN.

LYNCH, Pip
"Girls concepts of themselves and their experiences in outdoor education programmes." (1991). *Journal of Adventure Education and Outdoor Leadership*, 8(3), 27-31. (Co-author: Humberstone, B).

MARSH, Herbert W.
"A test of bipolar and androgyny perspectives of masculinity and femininity: The effect of participation in an Outward Bound program." (March 1989). *Journal of Personality*, 57(1), 115-137.

MAUGHAN, Jackie Johnson

The outdoor woman's guide to sports, fitness, and nutrition. (1983). Harrisburg, PA: Stackpole Books. (Co-author: Collins, K.).

McCLINTOCK, Mary

"Why women's outdoor trips?" (1996). In K. Warren (Ed.), *Women's Voices in Experiential Education*, (pp.18-23). Dubuque, IA: Kendall/Hunt.

"Lesbian baiting hurts all women." (1996). In K. Warren (Ed.), *Women's Voices in Experiential Education*, (pp.241-250). Dubuque, IA: Kendall/Hunt.

"Leading roles." (Winter 1989). *Women Outdoors Magazine,* 9(2). Published by Women Outdoors, Inc. Medford, MA. Excerpted for this issue from Truth or Dare: Encounters with Power, Authority, and Mystery by Starhawk (Harper & Row, Publishers, Inc., 1987). Reprinted by Women Outdoors Magazine with permission.

McCLOY, Marjorie

"Trail blazers." (May 1991). *Women's Sports and Fitness,* 13(4), 42-46.

"Far trek." (May 1991). *Women's Sports and Fitness,* 12(5), 36-41.

MILLS, Judy

"Women adventure guides." (April 1988). *Women Sports and Fitness,* 10(3), 48-50.

"Great explorations." (June 1989). *MS,* 17(12), 58-62.

MIRANDA, Wilma
Publications

"The history of camping women in the professionalization of experiential education" (1996). In K. Warren (Ed.), *Women's voices in experiential education*, (pp. 63-77). Dubuque, IA: Kendall/Hunt. (Co-author: Yerkes, R.).

"Women outdoor leaders today." (February 1987). *Camping Magazine,* 59(4), 16-19, 28. (Co-author: Yerkes, R.).

"The genteel radicals." (February 1987). *Camping Magazine,* 59(4), 12-15, 31.

"Working women in the out-of-doors." (Summer 1986). *Women Oudoors Magazine.* (Special Issue), 7(1). (Co-author: Yerkes, R.).

"Women outdoors: Who are they?" (March 1985). *Parks & Recreation, 48-51, 95.* (Co-author: Yerkes, R.). Note: Abstract found under Yerkes.

"Heading for the hills and the search for gender solidarity." (Summer 1985). *Journal of Experiential Education,* 8(2), 6-9.

"Women's outdoor adventure programming." (May 1983). *Camping magazine,* 19-22. (Co-author: Yerkes, R.).

"Outdoor adventure programs for women?" (March 1983). *Women Outdoors magazine.*

"The need for research in outdoor education programs for women." (April 1982). *Journal of Physical Education, Recreation and Dance,* 53(4), 82-85 (Co-author: Yerkes, R.). Note: Abstract found under Yerkes, R.

Invited Papers

"Women in administrative leadership in experiential education." Paper presented at the 19th International Conference of the Association for Experiential Education. (October 1991). Lake Junaluska, NC (Co-presenter: Yerkes, R.). Note: Abstract found under Yerkes.

"In search of a feminist standard for outdoor programs." Paper presented at the 14th International Conference of the Association for Experiential Education. (October 1986). Connecticut. (Co-presenters/panel discussion: Warren, K., Tipett, S., Mitten, D., Waller)

"Women outdoor adventure leaders." Paper presented to the Research Section of the American Camping Association Annual Conference. (March 1985). Atlanta, GA (Co-presenter: Yerkes, R.).

MITTEN, Denise S.
Publications

"The value of feminist ethics in experiential education teaching and leadership." (1996). In K. Warren (Ed.), *Women's Voices in Experiential Education* (pp. 159-171). Dubuque, IA: Kendall/Hunt.

"Ethical considerations in adventure therapy: A feminist critique." (1994). *Women and Therapy,* 15(3-4). Special Issue: Wilderness therapy for women: The power of adventure, 55-84.

"Empowering girls and women in the outdoors." (1992). *Journal of Physical Education, Recreation, and Dance,* 63(2), 56-60.

"Leader's language impacts participant's experience." (1993). *Women Outdoors Magazine,* 13(3), 9-11.

"Outdoor leadership considerations with women survivors of sexual abuse." (May 1993). *Journal of Experiential Education*, 16(1), 7-13. (Co-author: Dutton, R.).

"Research in outdoor education: Group development and group dynamics." (1992). In K. Henderson (Ed.). *Coalition for Education inthe Outdoors Research Symposium Proceedings*. Bradford Woods, IN: Coalition for Education in the Outdoors.

"The opportunities of homogenous groups." (1992). In R. Cash (Ed.). *Proceedings Journal*. Crested Butte, CO: National Conference for Outdoor Leaders.

"Throw a party: The hostess concept of leadership." (1992). In R. Cash (Ed.). *Proceedings Journal*. Crested Butte, CO: National Conference for Outdoor Leaders.

"Meeting the unknown: Group dynamics in the wilderness." (1990). Published by Woodswomen, Inc. First edition 1986. Minneapolis, MN.

"Healthy bonding." (Summer 1990). Women Outdoors Magazine, 10(4). Published by Women Outdoors, Inc. Medford, MA.

"Healthy expressions of diversity lead to positive group experiences." (Fall 1989). *Journal of Experiential Education*, 12(3), 1-8. Boulder, CO: Association for Experiential Education.

"Women's outdoor programs need a different philosophy." (September 1986). *The Bulletin of the Association of College Unions-International*, 54(5), 16-19. Bloomington, IN.

"A philosophical basis for a women's outdoor adventure program." (Summer 1985). *Journal of Experiential Education*, 20-24. Boulder, CO: Association for Experiential Education.

"Stress management and wilderness activities - Women's experiential education." (1986). In M. Gass & L. Buell (Eds.), *AEE Conference Proceedings* (pp. 29-34). Moodus, CT: Association for Experiential Education International Conference.

Invited papers
"Women as outdoor leaders." Women Outdoors New Zealand. (March 1990). Auckland, New Zealand.

"Women with careers in experiential eduction: Telling our stories," and "For men who want to more effectively work with women as co-leaders and participants." Association for Experiential Education International Conference. (October 1989). Sante Fe, NM.

"Leadership in a women's organization." Augsburg College. (October 1988). Minneapolis, MN.

"Outdoor programming with women who are survivors of domestic violence and rape." Association for Experiential Education International Conference. (1986). Moodus, CT.

"In search of a feminist standard for outdoor programs." Association for Experiential Education International Conference. (1986). Moodus, CT. (Co-presenters/panel discussion: Miranda, W., Warren, K., Tipett, S., Waller, K.).

"Working effectively with women leadership styles from a women's tradition." Association for Experiential Eduction International Conference. (October 1983). Lake Geneva, WI.

"Women in sports and outdoor recreation." National Women's Studies Association Conference. (June 1983). Columbus, OH.

"Meeting the unknown: Bonding in the wilderness." Association for Women in Psychology Conference. (April 1983). Seattle, WA.

NAVICKY, Diane

"The effects of a basic backpacking course upon self-reliance and mutual trust in an all-women's group." (1976). Unpublished master's thesis. Prometheus College (closed down): Tacoma, WA.

OSIUS, Alison

"Balance the scales." (May/June 1985). *Ultrasport,* 64-70. (Ceased publication).

PAGE, Lea

"Leading women in the outdoors." Masters project. (1986) Hampshire College: Amherst, MA.

"Women and outdoor leadership." *Women Outdoors Magazine* (Special Issue), 7(1). Summer 1986. Published by Women Outdoors, Inc. Medford, MA.

PARKHURST, Marlene J.

"A study of the perceived influence of a Minnesota Outward Bound course on the lives of selected women graduates." Doctoral dissertation. (Ph.D.). Department of Recreation (1983). Dissertation Abstracts International, 44/11A. (University Microfilms No. AAC8403751).

PETIET, Carol A.

"Neurobehavioral and psychological functioning of women exposed to high altitude in mountaineering." (1988). *Perceptual and Motor Skills,* 67(2). (Co-authors: Townes, B.D. & Brooks, R.J.).

PIRFMAN, Elenore

"The effects of a wilderness challenge course on victims of rape in locus-of-control, self-concept, and fear." Doctoral dissertation. (Ph.D.). University of Northern Colorado. 1988. Dissertation Abstracts International, 49/07B. (University Microfilms No. AAC8818574).

ROBERTS, Nina S.
Publications

"Kind of in the middle: The gendered meanings of the outdoors for women students." (January 1996). In L. McAvoy, L.A. Stringer, M.D. Bialeschki, & A. Young (Eds.). *Coalition for Education in the Outdoors Third Research Symposium Proceedings* (pp. 94-106). (Co-authors: Henderson, K.A., and Winn, S.). Note: Abstract found under Henderson.

"Wilderness as therapy for women." (May 1995) *Parks & Recreation* (Research Update), 30(5), 26-32.

"The outdoor recreation experience: Factors affecting participation of African American women." (May 1993). *Journal of Experiential Education*, 16(1), 14-18. (Co-author: E.B. Drogin)

"Portrayal of women in Climbing magazine, A content analysis: 1970-1990." Master's thesis, (M.A.). University of Maryland (1992). College Park, MD. (University Microfilms No. MA0043100001).

Invited papers

"Attitudes and experiences of women of color in the outdoors." Paper presented at the NRPA Leisure Research Symposium (October 1996). Kansas City, MO: National Recreation and Park Association Congress.

"Women of color in the outdoors: Involvement and culture." Paper presented at the NRPA Leisure Research Symposium (October 1996). Kansas City, MO: National Recreation and Park Association Congress (Co-presenter: Henderson, K.A.).

"Women of color in outdoor recreation: The role of culture and ethnicity." Paper presented at the International Conference on Women & Leisure: Toward a new understanding. (May 1995). Athens, GA: University of Georgia.

"Sports and outdoor recreation for women and girls: Issues and ideas." Paper presented at the National Recreation and Park Association Congress. (October 1994). Minneapolis, MN. (Panel presenters: Bialeschki, M.D., Mitten, D.M., Straw, S. & Thurber, K.).

"NAALA women speak out: Our vision, our voices, our values." Round table presentation at the first annual Native, African, Asian, Latino American Conference of the Association for Experiential Education. (September 1994). New York, NY.

"Portrayal of women climbers in *Climbing* magazine, 1970-1990: a content analysis." Paper presented to the Northeast Recreation Research Symposium. (April 1993). Saratoga Springs, NY. (Published in the *NERR Proceedings*, pp. 221-223).

ROGERS, Susan, E.

"Perceptions of selected outdoor recreational activities and their sex-appropriateness by physical education and recreation majors." Doctoral dissertation. (Ed.D). College of Health, Physical Education and Recreation. University of Oregon (1978). (Microform Publications No. BF692.2.R6).

SCHUETT, Michael A.
Publications

"An examination of the characteristics, preferences, and attitudes of mountain bike users of the national forests: A preliminary analysis." (May 1993). Final Report prepared for the USDA Forest Service. Pacific Southwest Research Station, Riverside, CA (Co-authors: Hollenhorst, S., Olson, D., Chavez, D.). Note: Abstract found under Hollenhorst.

"Refining measures of adventure recreation involvement." (1993). *Leisure Sciences*, 15, 205-216.

Invited Papers

"Differentiating between early and late adopters in mountain biking." Paper presented at the National Recreation and Park Association Congress (October 1994), Minneapolis, MN. (Co-presenters: Hollenhorst, S., Olson, D. and Chavez, D.). Note: Abstract published in the NRPA Leisure Research Symposium Book of Abstracts.

STERN, Barbara Lang

"Well-being: risks and thrills." (September 1988). *Vogue,* 178(9).

STEWART, William P.

"Influence of the onsite experience on recreation experience preference judgements." (1992). *Journal of Leisure Research*, 24(2), 185-198.

STRIPLING, Sherry

"Gender and the mountain expedition." (Fall 1990). *Women Outdoors Magazine*, 11(1). Published by Women Outdoors, Inc. Medford, MA.

WARREN, Karen

Books

Women's voices in experiential education, (Ed.), (1996). Dubuque, IA: Kendall/Hunt.

Publications

"Feminist pedagogy and experiential education: A critical look." (December 1993). *Journal of Experiential Education*, 16(3), 25-31. (Co-author: Rheingold, A.).

"Women's outdoor adventures." (1990). In Miles, J. and Priest, S. (Eds). *Adventure Education*. State College, PA: Venture Publishing.

"Professional outdoorswomen special issue." (Summer 1986). *Women Outdoors Magazine,* Guest Editor, 7(1).

"Women's outdoor adventure experience: Myth and reality." (Summer 1985). *Journal of Experiential Education,* 8(2), 10-14.

"Women in the wilderness." (1983). *Prairie Women's Journal.*

Invited papers

"Applied feminism: Leading gender sensitive outdoor experiences." Association for Experiential Education International Conference. (November 1994). Austin, TX.

"New directions for outdoor leadership: A feminist perspective." Women Outdoors New Zealand. (January 1990). Christchurch, New Zealand

"In search of a feminist standard for outdoor programs." Association for Experiential Education International Conference. (1986). Moodus, CT. (Co-presenters / panel discussion: Miranda, W., Tipett, S., Mitten, D., Waller, K.)

WASHINGTON, Sharon J.

Publications

"The relationship of the sensation seeking scale for risk-taking behavior in college women." Doctoral dissertation (Ph.D.). Ohio State University (1988). Dissertation Abstracts International, 49/10-A.

Invited Papers

"Sensation seeking and perceptions of risk of African American skiers." (October 1992). NRPA, Leisure Research Symposium.. Cincinnati, OH: National Recreation and Park Association Congress. (Note: Abstract published in the Leisure Research Symposium Book of Abstracts).

"The relationship of the sensation seeking scale and risk-taking behavior of college women." Paper presented at the NRPA Leisure Research Symposium. (October 1990). Phoenix, AZ: National Recreation and Park Association Congress. (Note: This is based on her Doctoral study at Ohio State).

WESELY, Jennifer K.

"Women, nature and violence: A deconstructive approach." Unpublished master's thesis (M.S.), Department of Recreation Management and Tourism. (1997). Arizona State University, Tempe, AZ.

VESLEY, Carol A.

"Caving practices, involvement in caving, and personality in NSS cavers: A survey study." (1985). *The NSS Bulletin; Journal of Cavers and Karst Studies*, 47(1). (Co-author: Bunnel, D.). Note: Abstract found under Bunnel.

YERKES, Rita
Publications

"The history of camping women in the professionalization of experiential education." (1996). In K. Warren (Ed.), *Women's voices in experiential education*, (pp. 63-77). Dubuque, IA: Kendall/Hunt. (Co-author: Miranda, W.). Note: Abstract under Miranda.

"Women outdoor leaders today." (February 1987). *Camping Magazine,* 59(4), 16-19, 28. (Co-author: Miranda, W.). Note: Abstract found under Miranda.

"Working women in the out-of-doors." (Summer 1986). *Women Outdoors Magazine,* Special Issue, 7(1). Published by Women Outdoors, Inc. Medford, MA (Co-author: Miranda, W.). Note: Abstract found under Miranda.

"Women outdoors: Who are they?" (March 1985). *Parks & Recreation, 48-51, 95.* (Co-author: Miranda, W.).

"Women's outdoor adventure programming." (May 1983). *Camping Magazine.* (Co-author: Miranda, W.). Note: Abstract found under Miranda.

"The need for research in outdoor education programs for women." (April 1982). *Journal of Health, Physical Education, Recreation and Dance,* 53(4), 82-85. (Co-author Miranda, W.).

"WIN - Towson university's women in nature." (Spring 1982). *Outdoor Communicator, 12(5).* The journal of the New York State Outdoor Education Association.

Invited papers

"Women and outdoor adventure: Kindred spirits." Paper presented at the Women's Studies Association Conference. (November 1993). Northern Illinois University.

"Women in administrative leadership in experiential education." Paper presented at the 19th International Conference of the Association for Experiential Education. (October 1991). Lake Junaluska, NC. (Co-presenter: Miranda, W.).

"Careers for women in experiential education." Panel presentation and discussion at the Association for Experiential Education International Conference. (October 1989).

"Empowering women leaders in experiential education toward pollicy initiatives." Paper presented at the Association for Experiential Education International Conference (October 1989). Co-presenter: Miranda, W.).

"The need for a national women's outdoor leaders' directory." Paper presented at the American Camping Association National Conference. (February 1988). Nashville, TN.

"20th century outdoor women leaders." Paper presented at the International Camping Congress. (March 1987). Washington, D.C. (Co-presenter: Miranda, W.).

"Women outdoor adventure leaders." Paper presented to the Research Section of the American Camping Association Annual Conference. (March 1985). Atlanta, GA. (Co-presenter: Miranda, W.).

"A history of women outdoor leaders." Paper presented at the Association for Experiential Education International Conference. (October 1984). Lake Junaluska, NC. (Co-presenter: Miranda, W.).

"Women's outdoor adventure programming." Paper presented at the American Camping Association National Conference. (February 1984). San Diego, CA.

"Androgynous outdoor leadership." Paper presented at the Association for Experiential Education International Conference. (October 1983). Wisconsin. (Co-presenter: Miranda,W.).

ABSTRACTS

ABROMOWITZ, Jennifer. (1977). "Women athletes: A reference document for a course on the subject." Senior Thesis. Amherst, MA: Hampshire College.

This study includes a detailed working document for teaching a course on the subject. Provides an overview of the difficulties and challenges of being a woman athlete. Looks at how women are being empowered by and making changes within athletics. Both conventional athletics and non-traditional wilderness activities are covered. Regarding women and wilderness the author touches areas pertaining to women as instructors and guides, program directors, and adventurers.

APPLING, Leslie. (September 1989). *Women and leadership*. **Proceedings of the NOLS Staff Conference**, 9-12. Lander, WY: National Outdoor Leadership School.

Discusses some of the social forces at work in society which effect women, and how these effects carry over onto NOLS courses and shape student behavior. Examples of topics looked at include: sexism, socialization, policy-making, gender roles and stereotypes and cultural norms. Examines factors involved in child development and compares females with males (e.g., self-confidence, achievement motivation, competition, bonding). Looks at the NOLS experience and it's relevance to women. "Gender roles and stereotypes surface with depressing regularity and predictability. . ." Provides recommendations for making a NOLS course work as well as possible for female students emphasis on the emotional climate to increase confidence, competence, involvement, use of language, and the ability to explore challenge. Provides a list of "conditions" for empowering women students.

BAKER-GRAHAM, Abigail. (April 1994). *Work with girls and young women at risk*. **Proceedings of a National One-Day Conference on Adventure-Based Interventions, and a Study Weekend Enabling Troubled Youth**. Ambleside, England, United Kingdom. (Available in ERIC Database, AN: ED378021).

This paper discusses the use of outdoor education activities with adolescent at-risk girls. Highlights the importance of women only groups providing space for identity development, relating to other women without pressures of mixed-gender groups, and exploring issues particular to young women. The Leeds (England) local education agency sponsors groups for girls at risk for substance abuse, nonattendance at school, or petty crime. Describes a "typical" group as 10 girls aged 14-15. The presence of a confident and competent woman leader forces the group to question preconceived images about roles and abilities. Although groups vary in length, minimum commitment of ten 2-hour sessions is recommended. The progression of the group is measured by effective and continuous evaluation related to negotiated aims and learning outcomes.

BEAN, Mary. (1988). *Women in risk recreation.* **Women in Natural Resources,** 10(1), 26-28.

Examines what attracts women to risk recreation. This article analyzes how adventure sports have traditionally been the domain of men, and how they have become fair game for women. Research suggests that there may be a physiological predisposition to risk taking. Interviews three women adventure program instructors. For all the women, in addition to mastering a challenge, the social rewards are among the strongest appeals of adventure recreation. Discusses findings of various research on *perceived risk.* Social scientists find that women who participate in risk recreation rate themselves as possessing traits viewed by traditional Americans as masculine. The author indicates that women who score high on measures of risk taking tend to practice a wide repertoire of behavior, rather than restricting themselves to roles traditionally reserved for women. The author quotes the director of the University of Idaho's Outdoor Activity Program (OAP), "women in mixed groups handle stressful situations, decision making, and responsibility differently than they do in all-women groups." He contends that when men are present, women allow men to take leadership roles and tend to defer decisions to them. When traditional social attitudes change, so then will leadership roles.

BELL, Martha. (Fall 1996). *Empowerment, competency and coercion: Experiences of pleasure and fear in a group of women outdoor instructors.* In B. Baker (Ed.), **AEE Conference Proceedings,** (pp. 28-32). Spokane, WA: Association for Experiential Education 24th Annual International Conference.

This pilot study engage New Zealand women instructors and facilitators about experiences of competent embodiment in the outdoors. A survey was designed soliciting women's experiences of "pleasure, danger, fear, risk and competency." This was distributed in a 'snowball' technique in September 1993 at a national outdoor instructors' conference. A qualitative methodology was employed using content analysis to sort and code the data into categories. Twelve categories were found; memo writing and hurricane thinking were undertaken to record linkages between responses and categories. Several major themes emerged: physicality, competence, danger, sexual harassment, and control. As stated by one respondent, "....the [physical/outdoor] experience stays in your physical memory and affects the way you feel about your body's power." Based on the results, the discussion notes that body memory work is an appropriate methodology to pursue further, "particularly significant to women in physical activity for whom the use of skill, force and space-occupying movement for pleasure and fear is an essential component of their embodied competency."

Feminists challenging assumptions about outdoor leadership. (1996). In K. Warren (Ed.), **Women's Voices in Experiential Education**, (pp. 141-156). Dubuque, IA: Kendall/Hunt. (Note: this chapter is based on her master's thesis).

An examination of the effects of feminist consciousness on the professional lives of women who lead outdoor experiences. Three women, plus the author as participant-researcher, engaged in a qualitative research study aimed at finding out how their feminist beliefs affect their professional practice, thereby enhancing their collective ability to forge new awareness through personal reflection. Through individual and group interviews involving these four Canadian women, several themes emerged. For purposes of this chapter, the focus theme is that "a socio-cultural approach to examining our practice in the outdoors contests the notion that anyone practices leadership -- or feminism -- as a generic role, abstracted from the cultural context and the influence of social structures. Rather than as single theoretical perspectives, leadership and feminism could productively be explored as sets of varied practices, employed to accomplish their political possibilities self-reflexively." The author also examines overriding theoretical perspectives about outdoor leadership and group facilitation.

"Feminist outdoor leadership: Understandings of the complexities of feminist practice as women outdoor leaders." Master's Thesis (M.Ed.). Department of Adult Education, Ontario Institute for Studies in Education, (1993). University of Toronto, Canada.

Four women who self-identified as feminist (including the author as participant-researcher), participated in a qualitative research study which examined the way in which their feminism affects their professional work as outdoor instructors and group facilitators in experiential education. Data were gathered through face-to-face indepth interviews, checked with the participants, and analyzed for emergent themes. Initial findings were discussed by the participants in a focus group as well as being analyzed as data. Results indicate that a commitment to feminism in the lives of these four professional, middle-class women of European descent does affect their work as leaders. "There is no one feminist approach to outdoor leadership. The approaches are understood as an ongoing and complex practice of surfacing contextual workings of relationships of power, and not the application of a set of principles or competencies." The four women in this study indicate the development of self-knowledge(s) as being based on *body, self and voice*. Regarding future research, it is noted that participant observation, phenomenological research and ethnography into identity, feelings and experiences in the body in field settings with women outdoor instructors would also build on the findings of this study.

BIALESCHKI, M. Deborah. (August 1993). *Expanding outdoor opportunities for women.* **Parks and Recreation**, 8, 36-40. (Co-author: Henderson, K.A.).

This paper looks at the benefits of outdoor activity for women, constraints to outdoor pursuits, and implications for leisure service providers. Issues of gender role empowerment are discussed and common constraints to involvement are examined. Major factors affecting women's participation more than men include conforming to gender expectations, ethic of care (responsibility and commitment to others), physical and psychological safety, and lack of skills and opportunities. The authors acknowledge the changes of women's roles in society but reiterate that gender expectations and safety issues are more closely linked to female participation in certain activities. Examples of implications for leisure service providers include: offering safe places to play, considering needs of women with disabilities in planning, offering skill classes that allow females to learn new skills without being intimidated, including more women leaders as role models, and addressing social issues that may limit women's abilities to participate fully.

We said, "why not?" -- A historical perspective on women's outdoor pursuits. (1992). **Journal of Physical Education, Recreation and Dance**, 63(2), 52-55.

This article discusses and reviews the extent to which women were personally and professionally immersed in outdoor recreation in the late 1800's and early 1900's. Examines the effect of the early feminist movement influencing women's involvement in physical recreation. Provides various explanations relating to struggles and barriers. Presents reliable sources (e.g., personal diaries, and other writings of personal experiences published in books by early explorers and adventure travelers). Reports on the involvement of women in early conservation and land preservation efforts.

The feminist movement and women's participation in physical recreation. (1990). **Journal of Physical Education, Recreation and Dance**, 61(1).

A historical perspective on the role of women and society as it relates to their development and participation in physical recreation. Discusses link between modern feminism and the effects of physical recreation as it contributes to women's accomplishments and successes in a world of patriarchy.

BIRKETT, B. (1989). **Women climbing: 200 years of achievement**. London: A & C Black Publishers, Ltd. (Co-author: Peascod, B.).

In the face of opposition from society, friends, or family, the successes of the women portrayed in this book rank among the finest rock climbing and mountaineering feats ever recorded. This research recounts a fascinating history of thirteen international climbers including their struggles and problems imposed by society as well as their achievements. Indepth interviews resulting from world-wide travel, along with information from extensive library research, and assistance from international climbing clubs are examples of how material and data was collected.

BLESSING, Brenda Kay. (1988). "Trait differences of women participants in selected levels of risk sports." Doctoral dissertation (Ph.D.). School of Health, Physical Education and Recreation. Ohio State University, OH. Dissertation Abstracts International, 49/04A. (University microfilms publication no. AAC8812229).

Purpose of the study: to investigate the differences and/or similarities of women who participate in selected levels of risk activities. The research sample consisted of seven different groups of women (all ages) who were categorized by the risk level of the activities in which they were participants. The high risk groups were comprised of skydivers, scuba divers, and rock climbers. The instruments used in the study were the Zuckerman Sensation Seeking Scale (ZSSS) Form V, Jackson Personality Inventory (JPI) and a background survey to obtain demographic information. The high risk group possesses more of the characteristics of sensation seeking than do low risk and comparison groups. Findings indicate that the HR woman may display behaviors that are: curious, contemplative, individualistic, innovative, indifferent, disciplined, venturesome, self-assured, directed, and liberal.

BUNNELL, David E. (1985). *Caving practices, involvement in caving, and personality in NSS cavers: A survey study.* **The NSS Bulletin; Journal of Cavers and Karst Studies**, 47(1), 51-57. (Co-author: Veseley, C.)

This research examined personality traits that attract individuals to caving, identified cavers preferences in caving activities and assessed significant sex differences. Data were gathered by means of a questionnaire distributed at the 1979 National Speleological Society (NSS) convention. Of the 275 surveys returned males constituted 70% of the respondents and females 30%. The average respondent had four years of college education, and was typically involved in the sciences, teaching, or engineering. Four personality measures were administered with the survey, including an activity temperament, sociability temperament, thrill and adventure seeking (TAS), and experience seeking (ES). Analysis performed included descriptive and frequency statistics, chi-square, grouped t-tests, Pearson correlations, and partial correlations. Key results pertaining to the female responses were as follows: 1) women reported going on fewer trips and owning less caving equipment, 2) women were more likely than men to have been introduced to caving by relatives or spouses, 3) women more often chose survey and horizontal trips, while men were more likely to prefer vertical, photographic, biologic, and exploration trips, 4) women were more likely motivated to cave for the "beauty of the cave environment," whereas men were more motivated by "personal glory" and "exploring the unknown" and, 5) females had significantly higher sociability scores than men (denoting a tendency to approach and initiate the need to re-examine the sex differences and determine whether women's participation in caving will increase as in other sports).

BURRUS-BAMMEL, Lei Lane. (1990). *Outdoor/Environmental Education -- An Overview for the Wise Use of Leisure.* **Journal of Physical Education, Recreation and Dance,** 61(4).

Focuses on the relationship between the outdoor environment and the recreational user. This article gives an overview of the existing needs for outdoor/environmental education programs, types of programs, political impacts, currents trends, a brief review of the expected and documented benefits received by participants and by society in general from O/EE programs, plus a few future projections. Page 52 includes female participation and discusses the growing attraction to all-women's outdoor groups.

Gender, sex roles and camping. (Fall 1983). **Women in Forestry,** 17-20.

The purpose of this study was to investigate specific camping behaviors and establish the relationship, if any, to sex typing (the degree of masculinity, femininity, and/or androgyny). The Bem Sex-Role Inventory was used to measure masculinity, femininity, or androgyny. A second part of the questionnaire contained a rating scale of 27 activities commonly associated with camping behavior. Questionnaires were sent to 900 randomly selected individuals in West Virginia in the spring of 1979. 577 were completed yielding a 53% return rate (of this, 52% were males, 54% females). Examples of results were as follows: 1) "Feminine" females and cross-sex typed males ("feminine characteristics") tended to camp less frequently than those classified as androgynous, "masculine" males, or cross-sex typed females; 2) The men in the study reported camping more days per year than the women; 3) When all 27 activities were considered, no significant overall differences between male and female on-site campers were found; 4) Significant differences were found on three individual items: males indicated more responsibility for both vehicle driving and fire building, while more females were in charge of meals; males were responsible for selecting the campsite; the only female-dominated activity appeared to be meals. The discussion notes that a greater proportion of campers compared to the general population is androgynous. Practical applications for improved advertising, marketing, camping gear and apparel needs to be considered in moving beyond the traditional images of women, and including women in the market for retail items.

CAMPBELL, John B. (1993). Sensation seeking among white water canoe and kayak paddlers. *Personality and Individual Differences,* 14(3), 489-491. (Co-authors: Tyrrell, D. & Zingaro).

This research study investigated levels and correlates of sensation seeking among members of canoe clubs. Subjects, consisting of 34 males and 20 females, completed the Zuckerman's Sensation Seeking Scale. Respondents also rated their: 1) paddling level, 2) highest difficulty level of the rivers they paddled with regularity, 3) highest difficulty level of the rivers they would like to paddle, and 4) anxiety level prior to put-in. Both female and male paddlers had significantly higher Thrill and Adventure Seeking scores (TAS) than the comparable normative scores. However, males obtained a higher mean score than females on the TAS results. Females scored higher than males on both the Boredom Susceptibility (BS) and Experience Seeking (ES) Indexes. It was noted that "one can obtain a low BS score by endorsing items that state a preference for 'the comfortable familiarity of old friends,' predictable outcomes, and familiar surroundings." Also noted was high ES scores can be obtained by selecting items that "state a preference for self-guided travel with no pre-planned timetable, friends in 'far out' groups and an individual style of dress."

CHENERY, Mary Faeth. (February 1987). *A Magical Place: YWCA Camp Westwind Creates a Mother-Child Camp*. **Camping magazine,** 23-26.

An article about a mother-child camp (20 years in operation) describing the importance of quality time in a safe outdoor environment. This paper examines the benefits and outcomes of the camp including: companionship with other women, special time with kids, time without household responsibilities, and more. Reviews a typical program schedule; provides a balance to participate in activities together and separately, and a balance between structure and freedom. Discusses logistical problems as well as costs, staffing needs, and special needs.

COLE, Ellen. (1994). *Wilderness therapy for women: The power of adventure*. Binghamton, NY: Haworth Press. (Co-editors: Erdman, E., Rothblum, E.D.).

A collection of 18 chapters examining risk-taking adventure activities in the outdoors for women as an alternative to traditional therapy. The contributing authors illustrate (both empirically and theoretically) the empowerment, confidence, and self-esteem women can derive from adventure and experiential activities. Investigates the symbolic value of wilderness accomplishments to women's mental health. Topics include: Body image and wilderness therapy; Therapeutic value of wilderness; Ethical considerations of experiential therapy; Ropes courses for women; All-women's river trips; Special populations (e.g., rape and incest survivors, welfare mothers, mid-life women).

DRINKWATER, Barbara. (1980). *Women on Annapurna*. **The Physician and Sportsmedicine,** 8(3), 93-99. (Co-author: Piro Kramar).

Report on research performed in order to prescribe a special physical conditioning program for eight of the ten women climbers who ascended on Annapurna. Summarizes the 18 months spent on intense preparation for the expedition. Discusses screening procedures such as pulmonary function tests; hydrostatic weighing; determination of body fat; tests of hand, arm and leg strength; exercise tests; and normoxic and hypoxic tests. Compared heart rate, ventilatory volumes and aerobic power with men. Conditioning program included weight training for each woman, in addition to a personal regimen of (almost) daily physical training tailored to meed individual needs and interests (i.e., ran marathon, ran stairs, bicycled, climbed hills with a loaded pack, and climbing or skiing in the mountains). Results of a questionnaire showed similar psychological responses as those given to ten top British male climbers.

ECKERT, Susan. (1981). *Through the eyes of women in the wilderness.* **The Creative Woman**, 4(4), 4-7.

This paper discusses the importance of wilderness experiences shaping the lives, wellness, wholeness and image of women as individuals. Studies reasons why all-women's wilderness adventures contribute to a powerful experience for women, and how perceptions are different than those of men. "Being with other women in the wilderness allows women to exercise leadership roles, to gain self-confidence by arriving at their own decisions, to take new risks, explore new opportunities and allow feelings of fear to come up and find support for those feelings from other women." The author also incorporates use of metaphor discussing the value of "seeing" the wilderness and "looking" at the environment through the view finder of a camera.

ENDRES, Christine. (Summer 1990). *Women's outdoor equipment (or lack of it).* **Women Outdoors Magazine,** 10(4). Article based on her Masters Thesis Research Project (M.A. Administration of Leisure Services. Aurora, IL: Aurora University).

Research conducted at the 1989 Women Outdoors Northeast Gathering. Purpose of study: to determine how female outdoor enthusiasts purchase their equipment; what is their awareness of existing outdoor equipment manufacturers, and what are the camping and outdoor equipment needs of the female outdoor pursuits participant? Comparative with other studies the sample group consisted of "mostly" white, single women with no children, college educated, and between 25 and 54 years old. The author discusses purchasing preferences, awareness, and behaviors. Findings indicate that local stores don't carry the equipment women are looking for, and that those catalogs most frequently ordered from (L.L. Bean, REI, and Campmor) sell women's products often made of "skimpier" materials, inappropriate colors, and higher priced than their male counterparts. This study indicates that outdoor equipment and outdoor clothing made to fit females comfortably is in demand.

ESTRELLAS, Anjanette. (1996). *The eustress paradigm: A strategy for decreasing stress in wilderness adventure programming.* In K. Warren (Ed.), **Women's Voices in Experiential Education**, pp. 32-44. Dubuque, IA: Kendall/Hunt.

This paper examines the use of stress and the related concepts of perceived risk, actual risk, and risk taking from both the feminist and stress challenge perspectives. Two key questions are investigated: 1) if stress is a consistent element of wilderness adventures, should stress be manipulated further or lessened? 2) if risk taking is performed from a position of stress, is there a tendency to jeopardize or enhance physical and emotional safety? An extensive literature review exploring stress research is conducted. A feminist model is based on current feminist literature on adventure education and nine conditions believed to be necessary for "eustress" (or good stress) to occur. This model takes its form in a spiral because of four intrinsic characteristics: 1) ability to expand and retract, 2) radiates from one center point, 3) each level of the spiral is an important part of the whole and, 4) circular fluidity.

"Understanding sexual trauma: A rationale and training manual for the experiential educator." Unpublished Master's Thesis (M.A.), Master of Arts Program, Prescott College. (1996). Prescott, AZ.

This graduate research resulted in development of a tool to aid in understanding sexual trauma and provide a means to discuss the impact sexual trauma has on the field of experiential education. Part one reviews the magnitude of sexual trauma in our society and how the field of experiential education has handled the issue. Part two is a training manual for experiential educators, wilderness instructors/counselors, and adventure therapists. The manual offers concrete information about sexual trauma (e.g., rape, child sexual abuse, incest, molestation) and the effects on experiential program participants. Additionally, the results of this study provides strategies for instructors on how to recognize and handle field situations that may cause distress to sexual trauma survivors.

EWERT, Alan W. (January 1992). *Fear in outdoor education: The influence of gender and program*. In K. Henderson (Ed.), **Research Symposium Proceedings**, Bradford Woods, IN: Coalition for Education in the Outdoors. (Co-author: Young, A.)

This study identifies and measures the situational fears and anxieties held by college students before, during, and after participation in an outdoor education program (at the Cortland College Outdoor Education Center, NY). From 42 different outdoor program trips, 380 students (recreation and physical education majors) completed the Situational Fear Inventory. Results show social-based fears (i.e., not meeting expectations of others, letting others down) were higher than physical-based fears. Gender differences were manifest at three points of measurement (beginning, middle and end), with females reporting higher levels of anxiety. Additionally, it was reported that all fear levels were reduced due to participation in the program; and, "in most instances, degree and significance of fear reductions were similar for men and women."

The identification and modification of situational fears associated with outdoor recreation. (1988). **Journal of Leisure Research**, 20(2), 106-117.

This study identified what types of situational fears were held by participants attending an Outward Bound (OB) summer course. The patterns of situational fears were studied from the context of: 1) what individuals were afraid of before, immediately after and one-year following their OB course; 2) what was the intensity of these fears; and 3) were these patterns of fear related to the variables of gender, age or length of the course. The instrument used to collect data was a 23 item Situational Fear Inventory (SFI). Of the total respondents 74% were male and 26% were female. An analysis of the variables revealed gender played an important role in numerous specific situations both before and immediately after the course. When a significant difference was noted, females reported higher levels of fearfulness than did males. Examples of situational fears which females reported higher levels include: lack of control, letting myself down, task too demanding, not enough ability, hostile environment, insects/venomous animals, fast/deep water, and not enough training. The items generating the most significant gender differences one year after the course were "not having enough personal ability" and "not enough training." Findings indicate that although some gender differences may be more pronounced when it comes to specific situations, females are more willing to admit to their apprehensions than males. The author contends there is a systematic bias in effect because previous work suggests females are no more fearful of specific situations than are males, just more prone to admit those fears.

Reduction of trait anxiety through participation in Outward Bound. (1988). **Leisure Sciences**, 10(2), 107-117.

The purpose of this study was to determine if participation in an Outward Bound (OB) summer course reduced individual levels of trait anxiety (described as a person's overall disposition toward anxiety which is closely related to the individual's personality rather than the current set of circumstances). The study sample consisted of 61% male and 39% female; the mean age of the respondents was 21 years. To obtain a quantitative measurement, a modified version of the State-Trait Anxiety Inventory (STAI) was developed. The instrument was administered to the participants prior to the course (pre-test), immediately after (post-test) and one year following the end of the course. A three-way ANOVA was performed on the data to determine whether gender, course length, or age had any effect on trait anxiety. Regarding pre-course scores, no significant differences were noted for these variables, however, for the follow-up scores (one year after course end) there was a significant interaction effect of course length by age. That is, adults who took a longer course (15-24 days) reported less trait anxiety than adults who participated in a shorter course (9-15 days). The author concludes that the findings of this study further dispel the myth that women are more afraid than men in the outdoors. Pertaining to age, differences in the scores of anxiety levels after one year may be the result of a deliberate attempt of the older student to become "less fearful and more self-confident."

FINKENBERG, Mel E. (1994). *Participation in adventure-based activities and self-concepts of college men and women.* **Perceptual and Motor Skills**, 78, 1119-1122.

In this study, the following hypothesis was examined: participation in adventure-based education can act as a positive catalyst for positive self-concept change. A total of 50 students (25 women, 25 men) enrolled in either a semester long adventure education class or in a general health class (control group). Each class had an approximately equal distribution of women and men. The Tennessee Self-Concept scale was administered to assess self-concept. The women in the adventure group scored significantly higher on two of the nine sub-scales plus total self-concept than did their peers in the control group. On the average (using ANOVA) women in the adventure group scored higher than men on the following scales: Personal self, identity, self-satisfaction, and behavior -- men scored higher than women on: Physical self, moral-ethical self, family self, social self, and self-criticism.

FREYSINGER, Valeria J. (1990). *A lifespan perspective on women and physical recreation.* **Journal of Physical Education, Recreation and Dance,** 61(1), 48-51.

A research approach which explains the physical activity involvement of women as viewed through the individual's psychological and biological status. This is also placed in the context of socio-cultural environment and personal and "group" history. Early studies are highlighted giving situational factors found to have a negative effect on the leisure time of women. Provides indication that many women continue to get little support if involved in physical recreation; their femininity may be questioned. Social expectations, opportunity, cultural norms, roles and preoccupations varying by age and sex influence current findings. How influences of social power change over a lifespan has yet to be looked at.

GOLDSTEIN, Judith E. (1983). *Women striving: Pursuing the physical challenge.* **Parks & Recreation,** 71-81.

A collection of 16 case studies about the feelings, fears, struggles, and vulnerabilities that affect women participating in sports and outdoor recreation activities. Personal journeys of overcoming barriers and constraints have placed an affirmation on past physically challenging experiences and how they have influenced their abilities in their present lives.

GRIFFIN, Elizabeth. (1982). *An interview with Dr. Anne LaBastille.* **Outdoor Communicator.** Journal of the New York State Outdoor Education Association, 12(5).

Anne LaBastille is a role-model for women interested in exploring the wilderness. Not only is she an important spokesperson for the ecological movement, she has transformed her personal interest in the wilderness into a political statement urging of us to treasure and protect our natural environment. Discusses her experiences working with co-educational groups and differences found in her observations. Looks at how women over 35-40 can be encouraged to explore the wilderness more and the potential role of outdoor educators for this group. Sketches the traditional roles of men and women being lessened through shared experiences in the wilderness.

GROFF, Diane. (1989). "The effects of an outdoor adventure program on athletic team cohesion." Unpublished master's thesis, (M.A.). Radford University: Radford, VA.

Purpose of the study: to determine if an outdoor adventure program affected team cohesiveness for a woman's basketball team. Conducted a pretest and posttest using a variety of research scales. Subjects were also administered two questionnaires. Categories selected were characteristics of group members, characteristics of the group, and situations experienced by the group. Literature reviewed consisted of group cohesion, development of athletic team cohesion, outdoor adventure programs, and adventure activities for executives. Findings support the use of outdoor adventure programs as a means of positively affecting team cohesion.

HARDIN, Joy. (1979). "Outdoor/wilderness approaches to psychological education for women: A descriptive study." Doctoral dissertation (Ed.D.). Amherst, MA: University of Massachusetts. School of Education. Dissertation Abstracts International, 40, 4466A. (University Microfilms No. 80-0934).

Purpose of study: to contribute to an understanding of how to design and lead outdoor/wilderness experiences aimed at psychological gain for adult women. The research describes ten structured outdoor experiences based on participant observation and interviewing. Summary of the findings answer four questions: 1) what is the range in form and content of the courses currently offered? 2) what are the commonalities and differences in goals and assumptions? and, is there a consistent "women's course or women's approach" to the outdoors experience? 3) on what basis do leaders make decisions about appropriate course design and leadership behavior? and, 4) given the process by which practitioners design and lead courses, and the critical variables identified in the literature, can a systematic basis for decision-making be outlined?

HENDERSON, Karla A. (January 1996). *Kind of in the middle: The gendered meanings of the outdoors for women students.* In L. McAvoy, L.A. Stringer, M.D. Bialeschki, & A. Young (Eds.). **Coalition for Education in the Outdoors Third Research Symposium Proceedings**, (pp. 94-106). Bradford Woods, IN. (Co-authors: Winn, S. & Roberts, N.).

The purpose of this study was to examine the links between past, present, and future involvement for females and perceptions about whether the outdoors was perceived as a gendered environment. Data were collected using 5 focus group interviews and consisted of information gathered from 36 women with varying experiences in their involvement with the outdoors. The sample consisted of 5 African Americans, 2 Asian Americans, and 29 women of White heritage. All students were between the ages of 19-25. Several conclusions were drawn from this study. Additionally, several aspects of grounded theory emerged including aspects of exposure to outdoor opportunities as a child, involvement in the outdoors as a result of and resistance to a gendered society, and contradictions between idealized attitudes and the realities of women's involvement in the outdoors. Some differences in participation were noted based on race, however definitive comparisons were not possible given the nature of the research and small sample of women of color ($n=7$). More research is needed in this area.

Negotiating constraints and women's involvement in physical recreation. (October 1995). Paper presented at the National Recreation and park Association Congress, San Antonio, TX. (Abstract published in the NRPA Book of Abstracts for the Leisure Research Symposium).

The issues of constraint in women's physical recreation (P.R.) activity have been examined by a number of leisure researchers. To better understand the influence of constraints, the foundation for this study was built on Bandura's Theory of Self-Efficacy. The purposes of this study were to develop a scale to measure the self-efficacy of P.R. related to attitudes toward physical activity, perceived constraints and the negotiation of constraints, and to examine how these perceptions related to actual P.R. involvement and energy expenditure. For this study P.R. included sport, exercise, fitness, dance, or outdoor activities. A 67-item Physical Recreation Perception Scale was constructed. The questionnaire focused on three aspects: attitudes toward P.R., perceived constraints to P.R., and strategies for negotiating perceived constraints to P.R. A sample of 502 females (age 18-83) were invited to pilot test the instrument. A total of 370 questionnaires were completed (74% response rate). Results supported the social-psych theory of self-efficacy indicating women who perceived greater abilities to negotiate constraints to P.R. through various strategies were more successful in P.R. activities. The data suggested as women feel more empowered to exert control over their lives (e.g., developing strategies to negotiate constraints to physical activities), they will be more likely to participate in physical recreation opportunities.

(Ed.). (1992). *Breaking with tradition: Women and outdoor pursuits*. **Journal of Physical Education, Recreation and Dance**, 63(2), 49-51.

Introduction to a special feature in this journal describes increasing female involvement in outdoor activities. Looks at projections and trends of participation. Indicates need for discussions and research to consider social responsibility for care of the environment. Mentions need for further exploration of how the outcomes of outdoor pursuits can support educators and recreators in assisting females to have positive experiences in the outdoors. Indicates need to expand investigations of the involvement of females who have not traditionally been identified with the outdoors (e.g., less active); "may reveal additional outcomes of the experience."

Women and physical recreation. (1990). **Journal of Physical Education, Recreation and Dance**, 61(1), 41-47.

A report of research from three perspectives: historical, lifespan development, and social-psychological. Physical recreation is defined as "freely chosen, enjoyable activity which involves movement of the body and includes active sport, exercise, fitness, dance and outdoor activities." Examines and analyzes women's participation using a liberal feminist framework. Looks at changes needed to create an environment which will encourage more women to be involved in physical activity.

Qualitative evaluation of a women's week experience. (1987). **Journal of Experiential Education,** 10(2). (co-author Bialeschki, M.D.).

This research was conducted at a five-day camp designed specifically for women. Purpose of the study: to show how qualitative evaluation may be used to analyze outcomes and to describe the elements of an outdoor experience that made it particularly valuable to the women participants. Qualitative methodology consisted of pre-camp interview, participant observation evaluation, and follow-up questionnaire. Findings indicate that women want to feel a sense of control over their lives and the roles they choose to fill from day to day. The data collected offers new insights into program evaluation. Recommendations for future research in this area include involvement of two observers to limit bias, use adequate sampling procedures, provide training for the observers, treat data collection and analysis activities as two separate functions, and treat conclusions as working hypotheses. Note: This research was summarized and reported at the American Camping Association Conference in Atlanta, GA in March 1985.

Viva la diferencia! (1987). **Camping Magazine,** 59(4), 20-22. (Co-author: Bialeschki).

Examines and analyzes how gender differences in time perception, thought, power, relationships, responsibility, process vs. product, conservation and exploitation, and leadership all contribute to positive growth in outdoor learning. Discusses how concepts such as feminism, androgyny, and personality theory have enabled us to see new perspectives. Focuses on the camp experience for use of examples and reports of supporting research. Looks at the female "system" as neither superior nor inferior to the male or traditional view, but as offering important ways of viewing the world that may be helpful to both men and women involved in planning, evaluating, and participating in activities in the outdoors.

Outdoor experiential education (for women only). **AEE Conference Proceedings Journal,** pp. 35-41. (November 1986). Moodus, CT: Association for Experiential Education International Conference. (Co-author: Bialeschki, M.D.).

The purpose of this paper is to highlight the benefits of women only experiences in the outdoors. Mentions some research data and related literature which helped formulate some of the theories and philosophies presented. Discusses perceptions of the outdoors and the relationship to feminist thought (e.g., freedom of choice, power to control one's self). Examines the advantages of women only groups, leadership styles and considerations, and empowerment perspectives.

HESSBURG, John. (November 1985). *Taking hold.* **Pacific Northwest Magazine.** Special Issue: Women Who Climb Their Search for Balance.

Profiles several top women rock climbers and their quest for adventure equality. Studies the relationship between women climbers and the effects of sexual politics of being "on the edge." Looks at issues still prevalent regarding misconceptions of women's capabilities (i.e., quoted in an interview with Jim Donine: "Good women climbers are expressing themselves more ably in rock than in mountaineering...women are not always going to be able to carry their fair share of [expedition] gear").

HOLLENHORST, Steve. (May 1993). "An examination of the characteristics, preferences, and attitudes of mountain bike users of the National Forests: A preliminary analysis." Final Report prepared for the USDA Forest Service, Pacific Southwest Research Station, Riverside, CA.

The purpose of this study was to obtain descriptive information about mountain bike users on selected national forests (NF). The project used focus group interviews and on-site surveys to accomplish the following objectives: 1) describe demographics of mountain bike users on selected NF lands, 2) describe patterns of participation (e.g., participation rates, opportunity preferences, patterns of involvement/socialization), 3) identify existing or potential conflicts, and 4) identify issues and problems related to information dissemination and collection. Questionnaires were collected on-site from a sample of 750 mountain bikers of which 696 were "usable" (15% females; 85% males). Additionally, using a high moderator involvement technique, focus groups varying in size from 10 to 12 members was employed. The discussion states: "confirming the stereotype, mountain bikers on the national forests tend to be young, highly educated, affluent males from urban areas." The report includes the transcripts from the focus group interviews. Results from data reduction techniques showed several reasons for participation. Although the report does not provide much detail on gender differences, one woman is quoted as saying: "from a woman's point of view, I actually wanted to start mountain bike riding four years ago. There's not many women who were riding then so I got into road biking. Not until recently have more women come into the sport of mountain biking."

Rock climbers. (1988). **Women in Natural Resources,** 10(2).

Eighty-four rock climbers (69 males/15 females) from four types of climbing sites in Minnesota and Ohio were selected as study subjects. This study compares and contrasts female and male climbers in terms of skill level, experience, numbers of participants and social contexts of participation. Researchers explore the idea that recreationists can be classified on a continuum of *specialization,* and that distinctly different participant characteristics, behaviors, and preferences are associated with each level. Behavioral observations were recorded in addition to subjects completing a short questionnaire. The author states that rock climbing may be perceived by both men and women as requiring a great deal of muscular strength if it is to be engaged successfully. Apparently a significant barrier to participation, women are discouraged from trying the activity; men tend to climb with men. While climbing (and other adventure recreation) may be perceived as "too difficult for women," it is concluded that this perception is undergrounded. The average years of overall experience in rock climbing was 5 years for women and 7 years for men. Mentions that because it is only in the last few years that climbing has become "acceptable" for women, they (as a result) have fewer years of experience in this activity. Based on the data, it appears that the main barrier to participation is not skill and ability, but rather cultural stereotypes and misconceptions regarding the appropriateness of rock climbing as a leisure activity for women.

HOLZWARTH, Rachel. (Winter 1992). *Outdoor programs for women: What they mean to women.* **Women Outdoors Magazine**, 13(1), 8-10.

Examines the relationship between outdoor programs and what women aspire in their personal experience. Based on years of experience, observation, and interaction with over 5,000 women, the author summarizes "foundational principles" of why women choose to participate in women only settings: Learning and experiencing for herself; Gender-free expression; Individual goal setting; Flexible itinerary; Supportive atmosphere; Appropriate risk taking; Shared decision making; Cooperation not competition; Women leaders as role models; and, Fun as a priority. The author uses results obtained from previous studies to supplement these principles.

HUMBERSTONE, Barbara. (1990). *Gender, change and adventure education.* **Gender and Education**, 2(2), 199-215.

An analysis based on an ethnographic case study of outdoor/adventure education taking place at Shotmoor in Britain. Observational data show interesting interaction patterns and forms of communication that contradict those that prevail in mainstream schools (e.g., girls' and boys' accounts highlight significant differences in their views concerning themselves, teachers, and relations with others). The conclusion suggests that the material conditions, social relations, and ethos prevailing within the case study setting affect the form and content of the overt and "hidden" curicula made available to girls and boys, providing a shift in the construction of gender identities and relations. Discusses elements of fear and lack of confidence as related to that which inhibits success, not physical limitations or ability. Evidence from this research suggests that the particular contextual features mediated by the Shotmoor teachers provided for a situation in which many girls and boys were seeing themselves and each other from a different angle, one in which images of what it is to be 'female' or 'male' were visibly challenged.

ISRAEL, Edie. (Spring 1992). *Treatment intervention with battered women.* **NYSACD Journal**, 23-30. (Note: This paper is based on her dissertation research, 1989, University of Northern Colorado, Greeley, CO).

This article reports research into the effectiveness of an adventure experience on women survivors of violence. Fifteen battered women served as subjects by participating in a three-day wilderness challenge program developed by the Colorado Outward Bound School. This study examined the effects of a three day wilderness challenge program specifically designed for survivors of violence on battered women by measuring three mental health variables. Participants ranged in age from 27-48; nine women were divorced, four separated, and two remained married. Instruments used were the Problem Solving Inventory, Tennesse Self-Concept Scale, and the Levenson Locus of Control Scale. Results indicate that the women perceived themselves as having an increase in self-concept, a more positive appraisal of their problem-solving abilities, and greater expectation that chance and powerful others would less likely have an effect on them. It is noted that researchers are still unclear about how battered women perceive and experience control in their lives. Further investigation with a larger sample size is recommended.

JAMES, Bill. (1988). *Canoeing and gender issues*. **The Journal of Canadian Outward Bound School,** 4(1), 14-20.

Examines gender issues in canoeing through distribution of an informal questionnaire to six self-selected women. Explores whether women and men describe their experience of canoeing in different terms, if women feel that males' use of the canoe reflect a masculine code of sport, and whether the canoe was symbolized in male or female terms. Respondents generally reported that they did not associate canoeing with the promotion of masculine code of sport. One woman noted several trips she had been on where "the men were pushing harder to go further on a trip, or faster, as compared with the women." In determining a sociology of women and men canoeing the author asked whether on mixed-gender canoe trips there was a role division of labor. Most of those responding stated "the labor was quite evenly divided." Additional comments noted "we'd find that some of the women did proportionately more cooking and some of the men did proportionately more portaging - but generally these jobs were shared and any unequal division of labor came out of individuals' preferences rather than an imposed division of labor." Regarding feminine values and characteristics of canoeing, statements were: "substitute cooperation for competition; the mentality of 'conquering' lakes and rivers must be defeated and canoeing enjoyed by both sexes as a sport for pleasure; it is moments of wonder, awe and joy during those quiet times on a canoe trip that I value most."

JOHNSTON, Brenda J. (May 1993). *Gender differences among intermountain west cavers, rock climbers, and hang gliders in relation to psycho-social dimensions of constraint to participation*. **Proceedings of the Seventh Canadian Congress on Leisure Research,** pp. 213-216. Winnipeg, Canada.

This report discusses the preliminary results from a graduate study investigating female involvement and perceived constraints to participation in caving, rock climbing, and hang gliding. A questionnaire was developed and mailed to 900 individuals from 7 states; 626 surveys were returned (90% males, $n=424$ and 48% females, $n=202$). The author examines the influence of social roles on these activities for women. Constraint factors for men included: a) would not be doing what my family expects of me, b) little or no support from family or friends, c) partner's preferences different than mine, and d) don't want to do anything dangerous because my family depends on me. Constraint factors consistently more prevalent for women were: a) risk of physical injury, b) lack of skills, c) poor health from illness, and d) lack of discipline. Additionally, two open-ended questions yielded a content analysis exhibiting responses such as "society condones fear and risk taking more for men than women, females lack upper body strength, learned helplessness, taught to be dependent, low self-esteem, and fear of competition." Results also show that "while there were few significant participation differences between women and men over the last five years, there were no significant differences in participation over the last 12 months. Furthermore, although this may not reflect actual commitment to family and domestic responsibility, it was the men in the sample that felt more constrained by family, household, and other social role responsibilities. Consequently, it seems to be a history of socialization in regard to "appropriate" activities for women, rather than current social roles, that constrain female participation.

JORDAN, Deb. (1992). *Effective leadership for girls and women in outdoor recreation.* **Journal of Physical Education, Recreation and Dance,** 63(2), 61-64

Investigates theories and functions pertaining to successful leadership styles and techniques. Review of research also connects with gender differences and similarities, and roles of outdoor leaders. Reports on socialization and expectations of participants. Looks at misconceptions and stereotypes which continue to exist. Provides several methods of implementing effective leadership and strategies for minimizing limitations.

Snips and snails and puppy dog tails: The use of gender free language in experiential education. (1990). **Journal of Experiential Education,** 13(2), 45-49.

This paper looks at the implications for use of gender-identified language and behaviors in experiential education. Discusses the components of gender bias and how "change is slow" (often not without resistance) to be more inclusive when describing both sexes. Several theories are explored, the bias in language is addressed, and steps to equality are incorporated. The use of language as related to "hard skills and soft skills" is investigated. The powerful effects gender bias has on both leadership and participation is significant. Looks at the notion of "words to actions" regarding how behaviors are also areas for discovery of subtle or overt sexism. By citing numerous examples, mentions that "until we get a handle on how attitudes are being manifested through language and behaviors in experiential settings, this subtle sexism will continue." Provides recommendations for improving leadership in this area, and tips for observing language exchanged between participants and how to deal with behaviors encouraged by sexist thinking and attitudes.

To dream the impossible dream: A leadership camp for young women in Iowa. (1988). **Camping Magazine,** 60(7).

Examines the development of a leadership camp for girls established to free them (ages 13-16) from society's imposition and/or stereotypes when both sexes interact. Reviews activities presented to enhance leadership potential through concepts such as values clarification, cooperation and teamwork, trust and support, respect and acceptance, responsibility, independence and positive self-concept. Looks at importance of discussing both women's and men's roles in society, and the strengths and weaknesses of both genders. Briefly addresses other topics such as group dynamics (relationships), non-verbal communication, and power and leadership.

"An examination of gender differences in perceptions of outdoor leaders by Colorado Outward Bound pre-registrants." Doctoral dissertation. (R.Ed.). Indiana University. (1988). Dissertation Abstracts International, 50/05B. (University Microfilms No. AAC8917750).

The purpose of the study was to examine gender differences in perceptions of female and male outdoor leaders by pre-experience outdoor adventure participants. Two questionnaires were administered to 147 female and male pre-registrants of 1988 Outward Bound School summer courses. One instrument elicited gender role information about the respondents, while the other asked participants to read written descriptions about hypothetical leaders and respond to questions about leader competency. Sex of leader and levels of competency were varied in the descriptions. Results show that all subjects expressed a preference for a male outdoor leader thereby exhibiting gender bias. Of the participants males were more stereotypic in their responses than were females. Male participants exhibited "stereotypical" responses to the dependent measure coping with personality clashes, getting along with participants, and teaching outdoor cooking; female participants rated outdoor leaders according to actual levels of competence rather than sex of the leader.

KANE, Mary Jo. (1990). *Female involvement in physical recreation: Gender role as a constraint*. **Journal of Physical Education, Recreation and Dance,** 61(1), 52-56.

Report of research examining the barriers to physical recreation as a result of gender-role conformity. Discusses how female socialization, through the influence of gender as a social institution, acts as a powerful constraint against women's involvement. Analyzes "appropriate" versus "inappropriate" behaviors, and limitations put on growth and development of women as a result.

KAUFMANN, Elizabeth. (July/August 1991). *Ascent of woman*. **Women's Sports and Fitness,** 13(5).

The author profiles the world's top woman rock climber, Lynn Hill. A biographical study, beginning with a brief history, which takes the reader deep into Hill's life as a professional climber, female athlete, and spectacular woman all around. Includes personal interview with Hill and quotes several of her colleagues. Discusses obstacles of stereotyping and how society still perceives the excellence of female athletes as a masculine trait. Mentions her physical and mental training regime and how Lynn "has proved that women can compete on the same level as men."

KETCHIN, Anne Forrest. (1981). "Women out of bounds: An ethnography of Outward Bound as a symbolic experience." Doctoral dissertation. (Ph.D.). University of Colorado at Boulder. Dissertation Abstracts, 42/08A. (University Microfilms No. AAC8200797).

This study describes Outward Bound courses for Adult Women (OBW), the symbolic mechanisms found operating in all Outward Bound courses, and their relationship to the socio-cultural contexts of participants. Ethnographic data was gathered through participant observation and in-depth interviewing. Forty-nine participants were followed intensively for up to two years beginning just before the Outward Bound experience. Other women - 122 in all - participated less intensively. "Successful analysis must consider that Outward Bound courses occur in a context of rapid socio-cultural change, and course advertising claims that the experience is powerful enough to affect one's life permanently." The symbolic event's relationship to both its general and specific socio-cultural contexts is revealed through an analysis of symbols as actions, mental improvisations required of participants. The author discusses that in the case of OBW these are seen to facilitate rapid socio-cultural changes, by molding values, attitudes, and perceptions in such a way that participants (white middle class women over 30) are likely to act in accordance with popular media portrayals of the "modern" person.

KIEWA, Jackie. (1996). *Body satisfaction and competence: Hand and glove?* **Social Alternatives**, 15(2) 7-10.

A posted questionnaire which included Likert scale questions and ample space for "free-form" [open-ended] comments. Responses to scales were summarized as frequencies, free-form comments were coded and categorized. The sample for this survey was $n=224$. The women in the study were involved in a number of adventurous pursuits and were from Australia and New Zealand. Significant findings indicate the perception of competence is a key factor in creating body satisfaction. "It is far more effective than a focus on how one's body looks." Results show that one of the most important aspects of participating in outdoor activities is the feelings of mind/body unity which the women engender these feelings.

The essential female adventurer. (January 1995). In C. Simpson and B. Gidlow (Eds.), **ANZALS Proceedings: Second Conference - Leisure Connexions** (pp. 116-122). Canterbury, New Zealand: Australian and New Zealand Association for Leisure Studies.

This study was both a quantitative (posted questionnaire) and a qualitative analysis of the free-form [open-ended] comments which were attached to the questionnaire. Population in the study consisted of 400 women throughout Australia and New Zealand, all of whom were involved in climbing, kayaking, or SCUBA diving. Reasons for participation were subjected to factor analysis, which disclosed seven motives. The two most important (highest mean score) were called "Escape" and "Social Interaction." The elements which contributed to the factor of escape included both escape to (nature) and escape from (family). The highly rated social interaction factor has not yet been reported in similar studies conducted with primarily male subjects. Constraints were examined through the qualitative data, and seemed to revolve around family responsibilities; the socio-cultural context; and the particular nature of adventurous activities, which are "committing, expensive, and time consuming."

KIZER, Kenneth W. (1987). *Medical aspects of white-water kayaking*. **The Physician and Sportsmedicine**, 15(7), 128-132, 137.

Although white-water kayaking is an increasingly popular pastime, little is known about the specific medical problems encountered in this sport. The purpose of the study was to better delineate the frequency and nature of injuries associated with this activity. In 1981, the author sent out 1,000 questionnaires surveying over 50 kayaking schools, clubs, and related groups throughout the United States. Returned questionnaires were accepted until the spring of 1982 and were analyzed according to the personal characteristics, kayaking experience, and clinical problems. Out of 211 total questionnaires returned, 86% ($n=168$) were men, and 14% ($n=43$) were women. Fifty percent ($n=20$) of the women had been kayaking for less than 5 years compared to an average of 12 years for men. The results and discussion highlight the medical problems reported including specific injuries and physical conditions rating from minor to serious. Regarding upper extremity problems, it was noted that although shoulder dislocations were not disproportionately common among women in this study, women may be more susceptible because of their generally "less - well - developed upper body musculature."

KLARICH, Catherine. (1995). "Gender differences in outdoor recreation participation in Whitman County." Master's Thesis (M.S.). Department of Physical Education, Washington State University. (University Microfiche No. GV181.3.K53).

The purpose of this study was to investigate gender differences in outdoor recreation participation within Whitman County, Washington. Three hypotheses were tested: Men and women choose different outdoor recreation activities; perceived importance was predicted to be different for men than for women; and, men and women spend different amounts of time in outdoor recreation. Data were collected via a mail survey. Of 1,200 questionnaires sent, 376 were returned in useable condition (response rate of 31%). Results indicate there were significant gender differences in 5 of 34 outdoor recreation activity choices, even when mediated by age (i.e., hiking, fishing, hunting, driving for pleasure/sightseeing, target shooting). Men were significantly more likely to choose fishing, hunting, and target shooting than women. Women were significantly more likely to choose driving or sightseeing and hiking/walking than men. Results also show outdoor recreation was perceived as more important by men than women, however, there was no support for gender differences in the amount of time spent participating in outdoor recreation.

KNAPP, Clifford E. (1985). *Escaping the gender trap: The ultimate challenge for experiential educators.* **Journal of Experiential Education,** 8(2), 16-19.

This article describes the nature of the gender trap by citing examples from related research. Discusses importance of fostering androgyny ("possession of characteristics which are considered to belong to both males and females") as a leadership goal. Addresses several questions relating to the dynamics of gender that operate in outdoor programs. Looks at women's separation from co-ed groups flourishing to form their own models of outdoor experiences without male attitudes/influence. Also, the author indicates the need for cooperation from both sexes to help each other learn what we need in order to be complete professionals.

KOESLER, Rená. (1994). "Factors influencing leadership development in wilderness education." Doctoral dissertation, (Ph.D.). Michigan State University. Dissertation Abstracts International, 56/03A. (University Microfilms No. AA9524962).

The purpose of the study was to identify those factors in a wilderness course that contributed to leadership development in wilderness education. A quasi-experimental, pretest - posttest with control group designed to assess the effects of anxiety on self-efficacy. Students from the National Outdoor Leadership School (NOLS) were subjects for the study (102 females, 129 males). Significant findings: 1) self-efficacy (SE) was significantly higher for all participants after the course; 2) mentoring had the most significant influence on female SE, and immediate feedback had the most significant influence on male SE; 3) anxiety before the start of the wilderness course had a stronger effect on SE for females; and 4) there were no differences between female and male self-efficacy scores at posttest. Results indicate the pattern of developing leadership is different for females and males. Additionally, overall results conclude women had a greater increase in their self-efficacy as a result of their NOLS experience than men. Implications for wilderness educators are provided.

Opportunities and liabilities of female instructors. **NOLS Fourth Annual Wilderness Education Conference Proceedings.** (September 1992). Sinks Canyon, WY: National Outdoor Leadership School (co-presenters: Byrd, C; VanBarselaar, L; Timmons, M; and Kearney, S.).

This paper is based on a panel discussion consisting of four female NOLS instructors who together share 800 weeks in the field. The panelists discussed a wide range of gender-related issues affecting NOLS, their students and outdoor education in general. Topics included discussions focusing on the advantages and disadvantages of mixed gender instructor teams, whether or not NOLS wants female instructors on every course, outdoor education and the family lives of female instructors, recruiting and retaining female instructors, and men and women in the woods together. A chart is provided in this paper highlighting statistics of NOLS instructors by gender over a three to four year period.

KRAKAUER, Jon. (October 1990). *High aspirations.* **Women's Sports and Fitness,** 12(7), 32-36.

Biographical study on Kitty Calhoun as one of the best mountaineers in the U.S. (among both men and women). Mountaineering is arguably the most dangerous and demanding sport in the world. The author mentions and profiles Calhouns' struggles exemplifying climbing as a sport in which 95% of the participants are male.

LaBASTILLE, Anne. (1984). **Women and wilderness**. San Francisco, CA: Sierra Club Books.

Examines the historical roles of women in wilderness living and activity. Part one explores reasons of traditional behaviors associated with fears and barriers to women's experiences. Investigates the experience of wilderness as a confining rather than a liberating environment as a commonality among women, in sharp contrast to the freedom men found in it. Examines factors leading to a recent and ongoing "revolution" of women entering the wilderness as a professional career and/or living environment. Includes case studies, observations, and personal interviews.

LAINE, Kristen. (August 1987). *The Litmus Test: What works for women.* **Climbing Magazine**, 107-115.

Designated at the "harness try-out squad," more than 15 women climbers from the Seattle area performed a battery of tests on selected climbing harnesses. The following questions were asked: 1) Was it easy to put on the harness? 2) Did instructions come with the harness? If so, were they clear? 3) Did the harness design create safety problems? 4) How did the harness feel while climbing, belaying & rappelling? 5) How did the gear-racking system work? 6) Was the harness well-constructed and well-finished? and, 7) The "Litmus Test" Could a woman climber remain tied into the rope while attending to nature's demands? The study investigates design constraints of harness manufacturers and misconceptions associated with equipment as related to needs of women. Analyzes various harnesses and their correlating manufacturer and makes recommendations to female climbers.

LEHMANN, Kate. (1989). "Integrating ethics and leadership: A journey with Woodswomen." Unpublished master's thesis (M.A.). The College of St. Catherine: St. Paul, MN.

This thesis examines the leadership/group dynamic model utilized (and developed) by Woodswomen (Minneapolis). Explores the relationship of this model and examines how it relates to effective, ethical leadership. Looks at stages in group development and, based on the responsibilities and activities, how the group leader responds to ethical principles. Concludes that leader effectiveness is possible when grounded in a coherent ethical framework.

Connecting ethics and group leadership: A case study. (November 1991). **Journal of Experiential Education**, 14(3) 45-50.

This article is based on Lehmann's thesis research. Theoretically, there is a considerable amount of work which explores the connection between effective leadership and ethics. In order to support this "connection", the author examines the Woodswomen model through her participation on a week long trip into the Boundary Waters with nine other women. Lengthy interviews, observations, and personal experiences contributed to the study. Six ethical principles outlined by Robert Terry (1991), were the foundation for this project: Dwelling, freedom, justice, participation, love, and responsibility. The author identifies the stages of group development as they relate to the principles. It was confirmed that "the ethical principles guided both the leader and the constituent interactions...and provide the foundation for a successful group experience."

LENSKYJ, Helen (May 1995). "Reflections on the female body, violation and empowerment in leisure studies research: The case of wilderness therapy." Keynote presentation at the Women and Leisure Conference, Athens, GA.

The purpose of this paper is to present a feminist critique of recent developments in wilderness therapy, with a particular attention to programs for survivors of physical or sexual violence. The author presents the benefits of recreation participation in the natural environment, shares definitions and varying components of wilderness therapy, discusses wilderness therapy in relation to the female body, notes several "power issues" pertaining to women's wilderness therapy, and offers reflection to the use of metaphor in wilderness therapy.

LOEFFLER, T.A. (1996). *The current status of women's employment in outdoor leadership.* In L. McAvoy (Ed.), **Coalition for Education in the Outdoors, Third Biennial Research Symposium Proceedings**, 107-115. (Note: This paper is based on her doctoral research at the University of Minnesota).

The study analyzed women's employment rates from 62 outdoor organizations to determine women's representation in the outdoor field. Of the programs administrators who returned surveys, 55% ($n=34$) were women, while 45% ($n=28$) were men. Statistical analysis revealed that women were underrepresented in outdoor organizations at the executive and management levels using a proportionality standard. Additionally, women reported lower salaries and higher gender-based discrimination occurences than their male counterparts. The findings of this study includes several implications for practice for outdoor organizations.

"Factors which influence women's career development in outdoor leadership." Doctoral dissertation, (Ph.D.). University of Minnesota. (1995). Dissertation Abstracts International.

This exploratory study investigated the status of women's employment in outdoor education organizations as well as factors that facilitate and constrain women's ability to develop in outdoor leadership careers. A qualitative study employing survey and interview data collection methods. The sampling technique used yielded the $n=103$ programs that were surveyed in this study. The response rate$=60\%$. Twenty-five interview subjects were selected through a variety of sources. "The presence of powerful male networks were perceived to be the greatest constraint to women's career development in outdoor leadership." Other constraining influences were found to be low self-esteem, gender-role socialization, and absence of early outdoor experiences. A list of strategies for outdoor organizations was generated from the results of the study.

"Leading the way: Rock climbing instruction for women." Master's Thesis. (M.S.). Experiential Education Department, Mankato State University, (1991). Mankato, MN.

An analysis of rock climbing instruction as it pertains to the needs of women. Examines the components of the learning environment while focusing on the elements of effective leadership. Discusses acculturation factors, multi-pitch climbing, safety and trust considerations, issues of body image, issues of fear, and risk-taking. Responsibilities of instructors as role models and benefits of all-women's groups are also discussed. Conclusion states that "rock climbing" instruction for women not differ radically from that experienced by men. Successful rock climbing instructors, however, must be aware of women's unique needs and alter their instructional style to meet them. Additionally, results indicate that in rock climbing situations, women typically differ from men in their socialization, their body image and their previous ("mechanical") climbing experience.

LYNCH, Pip. (Fall 1991). *Girls concepts of themselves and their experiences in outdoor education programmes*. **Journal of Adventure Education and Outdoor Leadership**, 8(3), 27-31. (Co-author: Huberstone, B.).

Comparative analysis of the implications for girls in outdoor and adventure education in New Zealand and England. Observed and interviewed girls aged 13-15 in residential outdoor education programs. Girls in both settings stated that their self-confidence had increased as a result of the outdoor and adventure activities.

MARSH, Herbert W. (March 1989). *A test of bipolar and androgyny perspectives of masculinity and femininity: The effect of participation in an Outward Bound program.* **Journal of Personality**, 57(1), 115-137.

The purposes of this investigation were to examine theoretical issues in androgyny theory by testing the effect of participation in the Outward Bound (OB) program on measures of masculinity (M) and femininity (F). Bipolar conceptualizations of MF posit that an increase in either M or F must lead to a decrease in the other, whereas androgyny theory posits M and F to be independent constructs. Consistent with a priori predictions based on the nature of the OB program, participation substantially enhanced M and had a small positive effect on F. The 264 participants were between ages 16 and 37, 95% were single, 75% were male and 25% female. Participants completed one of eight standard OB courses offered at one of four different Australian sites. Of the 23 groups, 11 were all-male, 3 were all-female, and 9 were mixed-sex groups. Instruments used included the Bem Sex-Role Inventory, Australian Sex-Role Scale and Personal Attributes Questionnaire. Results and discussion showed that participation in OB led to an increase in M for men and women that was consistent across the three MF measures. For both M and F scores, increases for women were greater in single-sex groups than in mixed sex groups, whereas increases for men were similar in single-sex and mixed-sex groups. It was stated that some of the benefits for female participants might be enhanced when experienced in all-female groups where women have more opportunity to take leadership roles and make decisions than women in mixed-sex groups.

MAUGHAN, Jackie Johnson. (1983). **The Outdoor Woman's Guide to Sports, Fitness and Nutrition**. Harrisburg, PA: Stackpole Books.

A thorough and comprehensive book about fitness for outdoor sports and how participation in those sports will keep you fit. Includes research relating to nutrition and injury treatment. Scientific methods of training for endurance and strength are discussed. Written with advice of experts. Adventure related chapters in this book include: 1) Backpacking, hiking, and snowshoeing, 2) Climbing and mountaineering, 3) Canoeing, kayaking, and rafting, 4) Ski mountaineering, 5) Female adaptation to the environment, and 6) Physiology: the strength of women.

McCLINTOCK, Mary. (1996). *Why women's outdoor trips?* In K. Warren (Ed.), **Women's Voices in Experiential Education**, (pp. 18-23). Dubuque, IA: Kendall/Hunt.

Based on an experience participating on a course offered by the Hampshire College Outdoors Program titled, "Mountains, Back Roads, Rivers and Women" taught by Joy Hardin in 1976 (*see Hardin elsewhere in this bibliography*). The author notes the reasons why women on this course chose to be involved on an all-women's trip. Investigates why, 20 years later, many of the reasons fall into the same themes and categories. The author collected responses to this question from a variety of sources. Although there was a plethora of responses, thirty reasons are listed regarding the question "why did you choose a women's outdoor trip?" It is noted that "many of the reasons relate to women's desire to escape the bounds and limits that sexism and gender roles have placed on women." Also noted is that women would still want to do trips with other women "even if sexism disappeared tomorrow."

Lesbian baiting hurts all women. (1996). In K. Warren (Ed.), **Women's Voices in Experiential Education**, (pp. 241-250). Dubuque, IA: Kendall/Hunt.

Investigates one form of homophobia in experiential education known as "lesbian baiting." Through the examination of two case studies, this chapter highlights the key components, negative impacts, serious implications and adverse effects on all of us as a result of lesbian baiting. "Lesbian baiting is the intersection of two forms of oppression -- sexism and homophobia.... such baiting is an effective tool to maintain traditional gender roles because the existence of homophobia has made being labled a lesbian a negative, discrediting action. If being considered a lesbian were not derogatory in the general culture, lesbian baiting would not hold the power that it does." Results include recommendations for taking action against and preventing lesbian baiting.

Leading Roles. (Winter 1989). **Women Outdoors Magazine,** 9(2).

Report of pertinent facts from *Truth or Dare: Encounters with Power, Authority and Mystery* (by Starhawk) speaking to a type of non-traditional leadership she calls "responsive leadership." The author of this article relates this method as "particularly useful" for leaders of women's outdoor trips. Provides guidelines for responsive leadership.

McCLOY, Marjorie. (May 1991). *Trail blazers.* **Women's Sports and Fitness,** 13(4), 42-46.

Report on the fact that until recently, women backpackers have had to use equipment designed for a man's body. The author discussed how, after much needed research, several companies are now making equipment with a women's dimensions in mind. Several backpacks, sleeping bags, and hiking boots are reviewed, and information is given on how to purchase a backpack.

Far Trek. (July/August 1990). **Women's Sports and Fitness,** 12(5), 36-41.

Based on personal experience and observation, the author discusses trekking and mountaineering adventures in Nepal. Reports on the essential elements of hiking in the Everest region. Examines the importance of the physical strengthening process and increased coordination relating to preparation of climbing high altitudes and rigorous terrain. Address questions to ask about guides and logistics for women interested in this type of trip.

MILLS, Judy. (June 1989). *Great explorations*. **Ms. Magazine,** 17(2), 58-62.

A historical report studying women explorers, internationally, since the 1860's. Discusses "The Explorers Club" (established in 1905) and, in the introduction, states that it wasn't until 76 years later that they permitted women to become members. Addresses the "Type T" personality theory (adventurous spirit) defined by a University of Wisconsin psychologist. Looks at the Victorian era and explains how the accomplishments (described) of several women were "buried treasures" until almost 100 years later. Mentions the Society of Women Geographers founded in 1925. Interviews several men, who have believed women are physically inferior to them, and women (i.e., Arlene Blum, Rita Mathews, Ellen Brush) affected by "twisted conditioning" of male attitudes and lack of funding support from corporations. Reports that, although sexism is waning, modern men still use the same old excuses for wanting to leave women on the sidelines of adventure and exploration: "women are bad luck; women menstruate; women need privacy to excrete; women have babies; and women are the weaker sex." Bear research and management scientists reiterate, however, that there is no evidence that a menstruating woman prompts grizzlies to attack.

Women adventure guides. (April 1988). **Women's Sports and Fitness,** 10(3), 48-50.

In-depth interviews of four professional women guides: Tracey Reynolds (California), Christy Tews (California, base camp manager for the 1978 American Women's Himalayan Expedition), Andrea Heckman (New Mexico), and Maura Daly (Kathmandu). Focuses on the commitment of the guides to each of their participants. The author studies their genuine concern about the well-being of their "charges" (participants) and a dedication to their needs. Cites examples from experiences during Himalayan treks, white-water rafting on California's American River, and backpacking on Peru's Inca Trail. Mentions how romantic bonding is more prevalent among male guides, and that these women guides (echoing the thoughts of other women interviewed for this article) insist "love affairs are a no-no." Looks at reactions of male participants to female leaders. Focuses on intense responsibilities from managing the logistics of hundreds of pounds of gear and supplies, to nurturing the many varied emotions which often surface during the course of a trip.

MIRANDA, Wilma. (1996). *The history of camping women in the professionalization of experiential education.* In K. Warren (Ed.), **Women's Voices in Experiential Education**, (pp. 63-77). Dubuque, IA: Kendall/Hunt. (Co-author: Yerkes, R.).

A case study demonstrating how camping women acted to define the first institutional expression of what we term experiential education today. Examines how first in the National Association of Directors of Girls Camps (NADGC), and later in the Camp Directors Association, women came to view their work through two contradictory interpretive screens: 1) they borrowed the gender-based logic of their male prep-school colleagues to craft a heroic reading of "the director," and, 2) as association founders and members, they deployed this romantic image of the woman leader in service of their status in "professional" organization.

Discusses reconstructing the education of girls. Concludes that female leadership in the NADGC made possible a form of association democracy through which women's aims helped to establish norms constitutive of outdoor professionalism. States that the rise of feminist-based women's adventure programs in the 1980s represents a new attempt to link feminist educational thought to activist social ends; the 1990s are witness to the breakdown of bureaucratic systems noting that more than one version of professionalism and professional association is viable and successful. Notes that many detailed studies are required before a full and undistorted history of women in the varieties of experiential education can be written.

Women outdoor leaders today. (1987). **Camping Magazine,** 59(4), 16-19, 28. (Co-author: Yerkes, R.).

The first study to provide research on the status of professional women outdoor leaders. Questionnaire responses of 130 out of 200 women outdoor leaders representing Outward Bound, all-women's groups, university recreation instructors, and primary/secondary school teachers. Briefly mentions the outdoor recreation movement and recognition as a profession as "established" and defined by men which women did not shape but 'joined' after the fact." Findings discuss motivations to be an outdoor leader, perceptions of women leaders, gender influences on career, and the most essential qualities of an outdoor leader. Strategies mentioned by respondents for future focused on maintaining links with all-women programs in the field and developing a voice in professional organizations. Note: This research was summarized and reported at the American Camping Association conference in Atlanta, GA in March 1985.

The Genteel Radicals. (1987). **Camping Magazine,** 59(4), 12-15, 31.

A historical study examining the early development and justification of organized camping for girls. Profiles Laura Mattoon and Abbie Graham as they exemplify the commitments and strategies of women leaders in the early camping movement. Mentions how they lend their own form of social independence to the task of expanding possibilities for others.

Working women in the out-of-doors. (Summer 1986). **Women Outdoors Magazine,** 7(1). (Co-author: Yerkes, R.).

Uses data obtained from a questionnaire sent to 200 women outdoor leaders. Research discusses employment conditions, gender factors, motivations, perceptions, and characteristics/educational background. Looks at change and expansion of roles played by women leaders, and indicates need to develop our limited data base on gender-related concerns in outdoor adventure leadership.

Heading for the hills and the search for gender solidarity. (1985). **Journal of Experiential Education,** 8(2), 6-9.

The author studies a variety of gender issues including the role of experiential educators and the need for increasing sensitivity to gender related anxieties. In addition to men's search for community in the outdoors, this report examines the search for a women's community in the outdoors and discusses the importance of a valuable link to women's outdoor groups not provided by the worlds of family and work.

Women's outdoor adventure programming. (May 1983). **Camping Magazine,** 19-22. (Co-author: Yerkes, R.).

Results of a questionnaire designed to identify programs around the country, determine what was being offered, and discover how women felt about the impact of outdoor adventure experiences on their lives. Aims to identify demographic characteristics of women participants, and investigates some motives for joining all-women's adventure experiences, as well as for seeking outdoor challenges in general. The participants in this study were predominantly single, educated, middle to upper-middle class women. Studies program content and touches on leadership components. Concludes that more women across the country ought to have opportunities and be encouraged to participate in outdoor adventure experiences in professionally designed programs to meet their needs.

MITTEN, Denise S. (1994). *Ethical considerations in adventure therapy: A feminist critique.* **Women and Therapy**, 15(3-4). Special Issue: Wilderness therapy for women: The power of adventure. (See also Cole, Ellen).

The author presents a model which she believes recognizes women's strengths as well as needs. This model respects individual differences, recognizes and addresses the power of difference between leader/therapist and client, and respects the natural environment. As adventure therapy has its roots in patriarchal society, and was developed for boys and men, this paper discusses ethical considerations of providing adventure therapy for women.

Leader's language impacts participants experience. (1993). **Women Outdoors Magazine**, 13(3), 9-11.

Discusses language styles, ingredients of self-esteem, impact of language on emotions and identifies four ways to deliver messages more effectively. Provides an example of a "the highway metaphor" developed by Jean Clarke which illustrates the four language styles and appropriate methods for more effective communication: *Nurturing and structuring* help build positive self-esteem; *marshmallowing and controlling*, invite negative feelings about oneself. The author notes that "as outdoor leaders, we have the power and opportunity to impact self-esteem by the positive and negative messages that we use when we communicate."

Outdoor leadership considerations with women survivors of sexual abuse. (May 1993).
Journal of Experiential Education, 16(1), 7-13. (Co-author: Dutton, R.).

Based on observations and contacts with women survivors of sexual abuse, this paper was written with outdoor practitioners in mind, with a purpose of creating an awareness of the discomfort and feelings that may surface for survivors during an outdoor experience. A review of literature indicates there is very little written about how survivors experience outdoor living. Looks at behavioral indicators and provides useful and practical information that practitioners could benefit from when working with programs whose clients/participants are survivors. Mentions that the strategies included can be helpful when working with women who are not survivors but have difficulty with self-perception, lack of self-esteem, inexperience with natural elements, or other abusive experiences. The experience of the survivor may be accentuated, however, and require greater attention. Focuses on issues of inclusivity and safety, self-assessment, and impact of natural elements. Suggests ways for practitioners to help alleviate some of the stress and reactions survivors may experience in the outdoors. Concludes that the overall experience in the wilderness can be positive and exhilarating, and contribute a great deal to the healing process. In the natural environment "she can find ways to feel safe, set clear limits and boundaries, and still experience a oneness with nature."

Empowering girls and women in the outdoors. (1992). **Journal of Physical Education, Recreation and Dance,** 63(2), 56-60.

Examines the relationship between life changes, positive experiences, and women's outdoor programs. Discusses motivations for selecting an all-female trip, and relevant factors contributing to feelings of "empowerment." Investigates benefits obtained from participation in all-female outdoor trips. Includes principles of the Woodswomen program design incorporating valuable leadership concepts and goals. Offers examples of participant comments reflecting on attitudes and experiences.

Meeting the unknown: Group dynamics in the wilderness. (1990). Published by Woodswomen, Inc. Minneapolis, MN. First edition 1986.

Examines and analyzes the process of learning experiences for women participating in outdoor adventures. Discusses stages of group development, the leader's effect on the group an how the establishment of healthy relationships aid personal growth and attainment of group goals. Through observation, the author has developed program components that influence bonding and suggests use of inclusive language to invite process.

Healthy bonding. (Summer 1990). **Women Outdoors Magazine,** 10(4).

What kind of relationship/friendship develops as a result of women "bonding" in the outdoors? This article answers this question. Focuses on need for women to feel connections and how such relationships are formed. Looks at results and effects of unhealthy bonding.

Healthy expressions of diversity lead to positive group experiences. (1989). **Journal of Experiential Education,** 12(3).

Examines effective leadership strategies for promoting positive group experiences on outdoor trips. Looks at recognizing diversity and people's fears about diversity, and the challenge of a group leader to encourage participants to express their perspectives and wants. Discusses the ingredients of success for the Woodswomen model citing examples from miscellaneous trips. Woodswomen, Inc. is an adventure program offering wilderness trips for women of all ages. They continue working to build a strong international network of outdoors-women.

Stress management and wilderness activities - Women's experiential education. (November 1986). In M. Gass and L. Buell (Eds.), **AEE International Conference Proceedings** (pp. 29-33). Moodus, CT: Association for Experiential Education International Conference.

Results of observation and responses from participants at workshops indicate that women do not like how their behavior changes and how their experience is altered when under stress. Examples include becoming aggressive, withdrawal, hostility, blame, impatient, neglecting personal care, more accident prone and irritability. Analyzes methods of relieving stress by dealing with the cause rather than the symptom. Discusses the value of taking risks in the wilderness as a positive challenge and a learning adventure, as opposed to stress which is usually more of a burden. Explores some common causes of stress during outdoor trips and how women can manage them in order to avoid unsafe situations. Concludes that by enhancing the positive aspects of risk taking, the negative effects of stress are decreased.

Women's outdoor programs need a different philosophy. (September 1986). **The Bulletin of the Association of College Unions-International,** 54(5), 16-19. Bloomington, IN.

Based on experience and research, this article studies facts that women react differently and have significantly different experiences when in an all-women's group outside traditional male society. The author encourages all outdoor leaders (of women's groups, mixed gender, or men's) to recognize differences in people. Looks at principles used on Woodswomen trips, for example: "women don't need to be changed to fit into adventure programs or 'taught' in order to be good enough." Focuses on the key components for programming within a women's philosophy as 1) set the tone for feelings of safety and security, 2) avoiding feelings of one-up, one down, 3) offering individual choice to participate in activities, and 4) avoiding a success-failure approach to challenges.

A philosophical basis for a women's outdoor adventure program. (1985). **Journal of Experiential Education,** 8(2), 20-24.

Through observational research as well as knowledge of societal and cultural influences, the author discusses the principles and attitudes with women's groups in the outdoors. Supporting research indicates that feelings of safety and security from the start are conducive to handling physical challenges and accepting personal decisions. Looks at individuals and groups participating in activities with different strengths and desires for sharing and learning as a personal choice.

OSIUS, Alison. (May/June 1985.) *Balance the scales.* **Ultrasport,** 64-70. (ceased publication).

A report on the progression of women climbers touching on a brief history of attitudes by the men who have observed them. "It is time for women to be judged on the same scale as men, not a patronizing, outmoded one." Provides examples of achievements from women climbers all over the world and looks at their battles to overcome being treated differently. Discusses strategic misconceptions about women rock climbers and mentions that, although men are naturally stronger, the key element is "strength-to-weight ratio." Has researched the history of women mountaineers and includes factors such as their smaller size and inexperience as typical limitations to expedition climbing. Despite this, the author keenly articulates the increase in experience of women mountain climbers and asserts that such feats are more mental than physical. "Many women do not realize what practice can make them capable of doing." The author concludes with a personal desire of seeing mixed groups becoming the norm, and hopes that some day special issues of "women in sports" and recreation are no longer needed for inspiration.

PAGE, Lea. (Summer 1986). *Women and outdoor leadership.* **Women Outdoors Magazine,** 7(1). Based on Master's Project at Hampshire College.

Due to lack of information provided in libraries, the author designed an informal, exploratory, and descriptive questionnaire mailed to 100 women outdoor leaders nationwide. Results sketch some of the issues common to outdoor leaders. Profiled some responses from several leaders. Reflects on disappointment with number of responses (24 out of 100); "if women outdoor leaders are too busy to support each other, then the issue of **time** should be first on the agenda to be addressed."

PARKHURST, Marlene J. (1983). "A study of the perceived influence of a Minnesota Outward Bound course on the lives of selected women graduates." Doctoral dissertation. (Ph.D). University of Oregon. Dissertation Abstracts International, 44/11A. (University Microfilms No. AAC8403751).

The purpose of this study was to determine how selected women graduates of the Minnesota Outward Bound (MOBS) perceive the influence of that experience on their lives. Out of 620 total questionnaires mailed, 269 were completed (a return rate of 43%). The instrument designed for this research consisted of demographic information; an influence scale (based on a six point Likert Scale); and other questions to determine if self-confidence, initiative, maturity, and the ability to work with others had increased, decreased, or remained unchanged. Open-ended questions allowed for expression of other positive and negative influences. The results of regression analysis and ANOVA led to the conclusion that the perceived influence of the course was not explained by and did not depend on a) the age of the women, b) how long ago the participation took place, nor c) the type of course the women attended. A majority perceived that the MOBS experience increased self-confidence, initiative, maturity and ability to mix with others. The author concluded that participation in a MOBS course is perceived as a positive influence regardless of the age of the participant, or the type of course attended. Additionally, it was concluded that the "influence" was strong and not significantly different among graduates of different years.

PETIET, Carole A. (1988). *Neurobehavioral and psychosocial functioning of women exposed to high altitude in mountaineering.* **Perceptual and Motor Skills,** 67(2).

Studied the effects of chronic hypoxemia upon cognition and behavior of eight women exposed to high altitude in mountaineering. (Himalayan climb : 20,500 feet). Results found that cognitive functioning remained relatively intact with only two significant decrements, complex abstract reasoning and word finding ability. Significant changes were found on all psycho-social and physiological questions. Feelings of acceptance of others and anxiety declined significantly. Physical symptoms were greatest during the first five days of ascent. Subjects' self-ratings of mental functioning were significantly better after the expedition than either before or during the climb. (Self-assessments were correlated with emotions and physical symptoms). It is suggested that complex cognitive tasks and psycho-social functioning be studied in more detail as these were most influenced by exposure to high altitude in mountaineering.

PFIRMAN, Elenore. (1988). "The effects of a wilderness challenge course of victims of rape in locus-of-control, self-concept, and fear." Doctoral dissertation. University of Northern Colorado. Dissertation Abstracts International, 49/07B. (University Microfilms No. AAC8818574).

This study examined the effects of a 3-day wilderness course (Wilderness Challenge), as an adjunctive treatment for victims of rape in respect to fear, locus of control, and self-esteem.

Subjects in this study consisted of 16 women, age 18 and over, who were "victims of rape" and in therapy, and who were referred by their therapists. Data was collected four times: two weeks before the course, one week before the course, the last day of the course, and four to six weeks following the course. Analysis of variance was used to examine the data. Hypotheses tested represented three areas -- fear, self-esteem, and locus of control. Results indicate that after the Wilderness Challenge course there was a significant decrease in participants' overall level of fear, fear of rape, and fear of failure. Additionally, participants reported increased self-esteem, including positive feelings toward their body, identity, and interactions with others. Results also show that although the women saw others and "chance events" as having less control over their lives, they had not yet internalized their perceptions of having more internal control. Also, perceptions did not significantly change in relation to the women seeing themselves as "good" or "bad" persons. Statistical data indicate that a 3-day wilderness program containing specific activities in a structured sequence, may be effective as an complementary treatment in relieving long term symptoms in "victims with rape trauma."

ROBERTS, Nina S. (1995). *Wilderness as therapy for women*. **Parks & Recreation** (Research Update), 30(5), 26-32.

This paper discusses how women can benefit from wilderness experiences in restoring mental and physical well-being. Includes how the wilderness, as a natural environment, can be a "healing place" for women in search of self and new sources of strength. Examines safety issues, challenges for the therapist, perceived and actual risks, and elements of spirituality. The paper includes descriptions of several studies in progress. Literature citing work of notable scholars is incorporated. Factors affecting women of color and multicultural feminist therapy are discussed.

The outdoor recreation experience: Factors affecting participation of African American women. (May 1993). **Journal of Experiential Education**, 16(1), 14-18. (Co-author Drogin, E.)

Although an increasing number of women are enjoying the outdoors and participating in outdoor activities, the representation of black women among these masses is relatively low. What are the factors contributing to the non-participation of African American women in outdoor recreation activities? In order to address this question, relevant research was synthesized, and interviews were conducted with African American women in the Washington, D.C. area. Based on a literature review and contents of the interviews, several factors were discussed pertaining to the non-participation of African American women in outdoor recreation: historical oppression and racism, stereotyping by race and gender, lack of role models, insufficient exposure to activity options, limited accessibility to outdoor recreation areas, and oppressive economic conditions.

"Portrayal of women in Climbing magazine, A content analysis: 1970-1990." Master's Thesis, (M.A.) University of Maryland, College Park, MD. (1992). (University Microfilms No: MA043100001).

Purpose of the study: to examine the depiction of women climbers in Climbing magazine over a 20-year period. Using content analysis, change in the quantity and type of articles was determined, as were identifiable patterns or trends relating to women climbers. The degree of recognition given to women through the amount of photographic representation was delineated. Gender composition of the editorial board, for all issues in the study period, was assessed ($n=123$). A brief description of the article was recorded along with key passages expressing how women were treated, perceived and characterized. Literature review consisted of women and leisure; women and outdoor recreation; women and the media; link to feminism; and content analysis. Findings indicate a clear under-representation of the coverage of women (e.g., number of articles per issue mentioning women was 27.2% with no significant increase over time; females depicted in photos increased 13.7% over time; and females were profiled on less than 3% of the cover issues). Qualitatively, the changing emphasis of coverage given to females, from passive observers to active climbers and expedition leaders, is indicative of greater recognition of female climbers. The prevalence of linguistic sexism was noted, however, throughout the study period.

ROGERS, Susan E. (1978). "Perceptions of selected outdoor recreational activities and their sex-appropriateness by physical education and recreation majors." Doctoral dissertation. (Ed.D.). College of Health, Physical Education and Recreation. University of Oregon. (Microform Publications No. BF692.2.R6).

The main purpose of this study was to determine the relationship between perceptions of selected outdoor recreational activities as measured on a semantic differential scale and perceptions of the sex-appropriateness of those activities. The eight activities selected for the semantic differential scale included: archery, backpacking, downhill skiing, fishing, gardening, hunting, nature study and rock climbing. A seven-point Likert scale was used to determine perceptions of the sex-appropriateness of the eight activities for both sexes. Additionally, respondents (58 males, 61 females) were asked to indicate four of the listed activities which they would prefer to participate and which they would most like to teach or lead. No significant differences in *perception of the activities* existed between male and female students, however, both sexes tended to rate all activities in terms of "stereotyped traits." Regarding *perceptions of the sex-appropriateness* of the activities, significant differences at the .05 level were found for only one activity--rock climbing. Both sexes rated all activities as "male appropriate," but females rated rock climbing as more appropriate for males than males rated it. Both male and female subjects rated hunting and fishing as less appropriate for participation by females. Backpacking was the most preferred of the eight selected activities for both participation and teaching or leading.

SCHUETT, Michael A. (1993). *Refining measures of adventure recreation involvement.* **Leisure Sciences**, 15, 205-216.

This study looked at the level of enduring involvement of white water kayaking participants. "Enduring involvement" implies permanent attachment or a trait rather than a situational feeling or a state. Independent variables were frequency of participation, skill level, experience, social orientation, environmental preference, psychological outcomes, perceived risk, locus of control, and sensation seeking. The level of enduring involvement of participants was the dependent variable. The *level* was also predicted by gender. The sample consisted of 82 women (28%) and 209 men (72%). Findings show females experience more enduring involvement than males. Additionally, men appeared to have different needs and preferences than women, and this needs further exploration in adventure recreation research.

STERN, Barbara Lang. (September 1988). *Well-being: Risks and thrills.* **Vogue,** 178(9).

Although current research shows that men more than women crave the thrills and adventure of activities with physical risk, more and more women are being attracted to these activities. Several studies on the desire for women participating in physical activities involving risk are discussed.

STEWART, William P. (1992). *Influence of the onsite experiences on recreation experience preference judgements.* **Journal of Leisure Research**, 24(2), 185-198.

This study investigated the impact of actual experience on experience preference of adult women ages 16-69 day hiking without children. Of the 72 subjects, 49 (68%) fulfilled the complete requirements of the research design. Three-fourths had graduated from a four-year college, and 60% reported household income of greater than $40,000. Data was collected through interviews (two female interviewers) both before and after the trail hiking experience. Hypothesis: experience preference will change between pre-activity and post-activity assessments to accommodate the actual experience. A seven-point Likert-type scale was used to measure preferences. Dissonance theory was applied to this study: "perceived inconsistencies, referred to as dissonance, are psychologically uncomfortable and need to be resolved." Results of the study were consistent with this theory. Subjects that achieved a given experience, reinforced the high priority for that experience in their post-activity reporting of experience preference. Conversely, subjects who did not achieve a given experience, were likely to lower their reported priority for that experience between pre-test and post-test experience preference judgements. "A shift in experience preference between pre-activity and post-activity reports may be due to rationalization ... [this] could be considered a coping mechanism allowing the subject to accommodate the environment thereby maintaining psychological consistency."

STRIPLING, Sherry. (Fall 1990). *Gender and the mountain expedition.* **Women Outdoors Magazine**, 11(1).

Observational research including interviews and analysis of three women and eight men climbing 29,108 foot Mount Everest. "Gender was the last in line behind such issues as survival and success." Discusses Stacey Allison's country wide tour speaking to groups at seminars, and as a guest on television talk shows. Reports on learned facts that not all women share her confidence that "they are strong, capable and can do anything they want." Also, the author discusses the fact that equality is still elusive for many women, yet when situations are equal (i.e., Northwest American Everest Expedition), they need to be acknowledged and celebrated.

WARREN, Karen. (1996). (Ed). *Women's voices in experiential education.* Dubuque, IA: Kendall/Hunt.

A celebration and collection of women's voices in the field of experiential education and a contribution to the dialogue about gender issues in the profession. This book includes a feminist analysis of topics such as historical perspectives, leadership, pedagogy, philosophy, therapeutic wilderness programming, language, ethics, spiritual empowerment, women of color/culture, and considerations working with women survivors of sexual abuse and incest. Included are examples of how women's experiences can contribute to the field as a whole.

Feminist pedagogy and experiential education. (December 1993). **Journal of Experiential Education**, 16(3), 25-31. (Co-author: Rheingold, A.).

Looks at existing intersections between two theories: J. Dewey and feminist theory. Provides a feminist critique of experiential education. Purpose: to encourage critical thinking about how experiential education practice benefits or inhibits the direct experience of women and girls. Explores the use of power in educational relationships. Discusses the value of personal experience from the perspective of feminist educators. Offers suggestions about ways which feminist pedagogy can embrace, inform, and strengthen the learning, teaching, and practice of experiential education.

Women's outdoor adventures: Myth and reality. (1985). **Journal of Experiential Education,** 8(2), 10-14.

Examines and analyzes adventure programming from a feminist perspective through exploration of several myths which have typified a women's adventure experience. Discusses how these myths have served as barriers for women at various stages in their pursuit of meaningful outdoor challenges.

WASHINGTON, Sharon J. (1992). "Sensation seeking and perceptions of risk of African American skiers." *Book of Abstracts from the Leisure Research Symposium*, National Recreation and Park Association, National Congress, Cincinnati, OH.

The purpose of this study was to determine if there was a relationship between the Zuckerman Sensation Seeking Scale, and perceptions of self and skiing as "risky" for African Americans already engaged in a high risk recreational activity (downhill skiing). Respondents to a questionnaire consisted of 73 African Americans ($n = 38$ women, 34 men). Analysis of Variance (ANOVA) was used to treat the data of the study. Respondents who cited personal interest as the motivation achieved a mean score far higher than those who began skiing for social reasons. The second highest motivator, however, was attributed to family and/or friends. Subjects were asked whether or not they agreed or disagreed with the statement: "most African Americans view skiing as a [outdoor] sport for Whites." The responses were 26.8% ($n=19$) in agreement, while 73.2% ($n=52$) disagreed. The author notes that "African American skiers on vacation don't have a desire to participate in research, thought the survey was too long, and are skeptical about being researched."

"The relationship of the sensation seeking scale for risk-taking behavior in college women." Doctoral dissertation, (Ph.D.). Ohio State University, (1988). Dissertation Abstracts International, 49/10-A.

The purpose of the study was to determine if there was a relationship between the Zuckerman Sensation Seeking Scale (ZSSS) and physical risk-taking behavior. The scale was used to test a sample of 61 women enrolled in an introductory women's studies course at Ohio State. Subjects: 49 Euro-Americans, 10 African Americans, 1 Asian, 1 Hispanic. The activity used in the study was a "trapeze jump." Subjects were scored as to whether they jumped or not. Multiple regression and an f-test were utilized to treat the data. Results indicated there was no relationship between ZSSS scores and physical risk-taking behavior. There was, however, a significant relationship between scores from the ZSSS and the factor of race. Subjects of color ($n=12$) reported significantly lower means on the "thrill and adventure," and "disinhibition" sub-scales than whites. Tables representing the means and standard deviations are presented indicating the ZSSS and predictors.

WESELY, Jennifer, K. (1997). "Women, nature and violence." Unpublished Master's Thesis, (M.S.). Arizona State University, Tempe, AZ.

This study deconstructed the patriarchial paradigm in terms of its destructive effects on women in their relationship to nature and physical activity. Eight in-depth interviews were conducted at a domestic violence shelter in Arizona with females who were survivors of an abusive relationship. Information obtained revolved around three broad topics: female identity/psyche, female body, and nature. Findings revealed the depth to which the dominant ideology and dualistic thought affected the perspectives of these survivors of domestic violence. From these case studies, the women described a systematic identity fragmentation throughout the abusive relationship in which they felt they lost control of their physical self. During interviews, several of the women credited sport or other physical activity with being vital to their reconnection with their body after separating from their abuser. They described "escaping to the outdoors" during their abusive relationships (e.g., one woman elaborated upon her first camping experience, occuring two months after separation from her abuser, as pivotal in her healing process). The women all expressed a close kinship with nature through perceptions of common feminine traits, such as reproduction and nurturing. The interviewees identified ways in which physical activity (e.g., walking, camping, outdoor sports) allowed them to reconnect with their physical self and rebuild their female identity, and nature was explored as a means of healing for the women through the ecofeminist recognition of all living things as sacred.

YERKES, Rita. (October 1991). "Women in Administrative Leadership in Experiential Education." (Cassette Recording No. 108; produced by Goodkind of Sound). Lake Junaluska, NC: Association for Experiential Education 19th International Conference. (Co-presenter: Miranda, W.).

Discusses relationships of women and authority, and typical problems and dilemmas for women in administration. Explores methods of implementing various strategies for effective management. Communicates the importance of 1) understanding the type of organization in which one is employed; 2) effective use of language; and 3) knowledge of needs and wants of self and employer. Examines characteristics of a quality administrator and the role of feedback within an agency. Conclusion provides insight encouraging women in administration to take risks and accept results. Emphasis on networking and maintaining dignity in all endeavors.

Women outdoors: Who are they? (March 1985). **Parks and Recreation**, 48-51, 95. (Co-author: Miranda, W.).

From survey research this study looks at what motivates a women's interest in adventure experiences and why they seek these experiences in all-women groups. Discusses how such experiences influence the respondents in their daily lives. Reports from findings indicate that society must move beyond the misconception that there is no need for all-women's outdoor educational or leisure experiences. Women in the study, supporting research, indicate the need is very "real." Also, discusses need for women leaders as role models.

WIN: Towson university's women in nature. (Spring 1982). **Outdoor Communicator**, 12(5). The Journal of the New York State Outdoor Education Association.

Studies Towson University's (Baltimore, MD) first course offering in its "WIN--Women in Nature Program;" an informal outdoor education program designed for women over 25. Discusses this environment as a neutral place combined with skilled female outdoor leaders who understand the anxiety imposed by society that women have experienced about their physical ability, role expectations, and danger in seeking adventure, and how this creates the context for self-discovery. Looks at suggestions for other programs which include course offerings for females. Suggests using female role models to encourage adventure, hire and train program staff with care, provide quality equipment, utilize public relations, encourage participant questions and evaluate the program.

The need for research in outdoor education programs for women. (1982). **Journal of Physical Education, Recreation and Dance,** 53(4), 82-85.

Examines the issues which need to be addressed. Suggests methods of research. Looks at current support and experimentation for women's participation in and desire for adventure experiences. Offers several hypotheses to be tested and potential consequences of such research (i.e., to increase program effectiveness and broaden the theoretical base of adventure education). Covers the motivations and raises questions about preferences for exclusively female groups.

APPENDIX

APPENDIX

Nina S. Roberts, M.A.

A Guide to Women's Studies in the Outdoors:
Review of Literature and Research with Annotated Bibliography

GOALS

1. To provide a resource which would be instrumental in keeping research for women and adventure in the outdoors active and alive.

2. Compile an annotated bibliography of studies to assist persons interested with understanding and connecting the relationship between women's activities in the outdoors, to their status in and contributions to society.

3. Provide an abstract, annotation, or summary of findings with each reference.

4. Furnish a report which will offer expedience in referencing a list of international works cited for future research on women and adventure activities.

5. Identify the value of having a compilation of research studies, papers, and reports on gender differences in the outdoors.

6. Contribute to the emerging discipline of women in experiential education and physical recreation in the natural environment as it relates to the growth of studies on women and leisure as a whole.

OBJECTIVES

1. To compile a record of published and unpublished papers, theses, dissertations and empirical research studies in order to give students, practitioners and educators the increased recognition they deserve, as well as to assist with current and future research on women and adventure in the outdoors internationally.

2. To be used as a resource for women to view their lives as open to as many options that will enable them to adapt to a wide variety of possible career/leisure opportunities in the outdoors.

3. To have direct access to a multitude and variety of studies which will embody successes and constraints, a history of what has been confronted by women, and where they might be headed.

4. To provide researchers, and other persons interested, with a list of support literature in order to perform replicative studies as well as opportunities for new research.

5. To continue to show the importance of studying women in the outdoors/wilderness; such research is both a significant asset of and a possible deficit in the lives of women who are interested, yet unaware of life benefits or who do not have ample access of opportunities available to them.

6. To offer an essential resource for professionals and researchers as a networking tool to share information and related efforts for a multitude of purposes.

Women's Studies in the Outdoors
Review of Research with Annotated Bibliography

In the space below please provide me with names of individuals who have completed a study, are in the process of conducting research, or have written a paper, thesis, or dissertation related to this topic. I will send them a questionnaire, add them to my data base, and include them in updated editions. Please write legibly and provide as much information as you can.

Name _____

Address _____

City, State, Zip _____

Telephone _____

Name _____

Address _____

City, State, Zip _____

Telephone _____

Name _____

Address _____

City, State, Zip _____

Telephone _____

Name _____

Address _____

City, State, Zip _____

Telephone _____

Please return this form to: Nina Roberts, 9703 47th Place, College Park, MD 20740-1470

Women's Studies in the Outdoors -- Questionnaire

PLEASE type or print clearly! I would also appreciate receiving
a copy of your manuscript/paper, or an abstract, in order to annotate
or summarize your work.

Name _____

Address _____

City, State, Zip _____

Telephone _____

FAX _____

E-Mail _____

Title of Work
Completed or
In Progress _____

Please indicate the primary focus of your study. If multiple subject
areas are included please check all that apply:

_____ Leadership   _____ Gender issues   _____ Role models

_____ Ethics   _____ Learning styles   _____ Current trends

_____ Case study   _____ Social constraints   _____ Economics

_____ Equipment   _____ Ethnic/cultural   _____ Disability

_____ Historical   _____ Feminist framework   _____ Theory

_____ Physiology   _____ Group dynamics   _____ Other (explain)

Please return this form to: Nina Roberts, 9703 47th Place, College Park, MD 20740-1470